Praise for
John Livingston's Healing Work

"John has helped me connect with my past, understand the source of my insecurities, and work with this awareness to face everyday life as a more complete person."
— *Andreas Adamec, Graphic Artist*

"My family and I have received a special gift — a new chance in life. Our ability to use our free-will choices has greatly improved our lives both individually and together… collectively, there's much more harmony and peace."
— *Michelle Tamura, Reiki Practitioner*

"By showing me that invisible enemies were affecting my life, and that the condemning voice in my head was not always my own, John has given me a new level of consciousness."
— *Colleen O'Halloran, The May Institute*

"Working with John has changed my life profoundly. As I've learned to trust my intuition and to know that I have the power to heal and protect myself, the element of fear has disappeared."
— *Nila Bornstein, Australia*

'After working with John for only a few months… I've changed and grown more than I ever thought possible. I'm a much happier, more well-rounded person."
— *David Dennis, Voice artist, actor*

'I thank God for John Livingston! His work has helped me recognize hidden strengths and abilities and find my true purpose in life. I feel blessed to know him."
— *Lane Lenhart, Calif.*

'John has brought indescribable love and light. I've forgiven and let go of traumas that have been with me since before I could walk. Heavy layers of darkness have been lifted, and I can live my life without tormenting fear."
— *Kerry Barstad, Calif.*

Adversaries Walk Among Us

A Guide to the History, Nature, and Removal of Possessing Demons and Spirits

John G. Livingston, M.A.

LOST
COAST
PRESS

Adversaries Walk Among Us
Copyright © 2004 by John G. Livingston

Lost Coast Press
155 Cypress Street
Fort Bragg, CA 95437
(800) 773-7782
www.cypresshouse.com

Cover art: woodcut from *Biblia Pauperum*, 1440

Library of Congress Cataloging-in-Publication Data
Livingston, John G., 1934-
   Adversaries walk among us : a guide to the history, nature, and removal of possessing demons and spirits / John G. Livingston.-- 1st ed.
      p. cm.
Includes bibliographical references and index.
   ISBN 1-882897-80-3 (pbk. : alk. paper)
   1. Exorcism. 2. Demoniac possession. I. Title.
BF1559.L58 2004
133.4'27--dc22
2003028156

Printed in the USA

2 4 6 8 9 7 5 3 1

For my adversaries
and friends
who teach me
what I need to know.

Permissions

Warning and Disclaimer

The overriding purpose of this book is to provide information about the historical and present nature of demons, spirits, dark beings, and the dark forces. Neither the author nor the publisher are providing medical or legal or other professional services to the reader. Suggestions are made in the book for spiritual healing and personal protection, including a script to be read for self-help, with readers' intent to remove any parasitic spirit entities and/or demons from association with their energetic bodies. Whether this script "works" to provide relief from any emotional and physical symptoms held by the reader depends on many factors, including faith, lack (even momentary) of fear, a belief in and connection with a spiritual force and power of the universe known to many as God, and, of course, whether the symptoms have their root cause in parasitic entities and demons.

The work in this book is spiritual in nature, not medical or religious, and deals primarily with impairments to the subtle energy body that interpenetrates and surrounds the physical body.

Only qualified medical doctors are licensed to diagnose and cure disease. Anyone with symptoms of unknown cause is advised to consult with a competent doctor to determine whether medical action is indicated. However, in no case should an individual give his or her personal power of free-will choice over to any other individual, regardless of social pressures or pronouncements they make about the absolute nature of disease.

Foreword

The easiest way to describe my life? I was a twenty-one-year-old train wreck. I had always known what I wanted: a "normal" life; that is, a social life, a stable address, decent family interaction and support, and the kinds of things most people enjoy and take for granted. More than anything, I wanted to pursue my dream of becoming an animator. You might think these two desires would be easy enough to achieve, but something was horribly wrong with me.

Several people and schools have told me that I'm a very intelligent person, and I believed them. Many smart people have little trouble keeping a decent social life, a steady job, and the like, but I couldn't. I had no physical or mental handicaps to prevent me from holding on to a semblance of a normal life. I didn't come from the most supportive family, but they were financially well off. I didn't go to the best schools in the city, but I went to very good ones with fine teachers. I was never the popular kid in class, but I wasn't the nerd or the clown. I didn't make the honor roll every semester, but I didn't flunk out. Considered on the good side of average, or slightly above it, I should have been generally happy.

That wasn't the case. Every little thing would send me into an emotional turmoil that I couldn't cope with. Family problems and lack of many real friends killed any hope of a social life. When I left high school, I could never keep a job or support myself for any length of time. I'd seen a few therapists, but they didn't help much, wrote me off as depressed, did nothing about it, and that was the end of it. There always seemed to be issues, insignificant to everyone else, and no one could understand why I reacted to everything so emotionally, why seemingly impossible things would happen at the worst times, ruin my plans, and send me into a funk for months. I just couldn't keep a life together; no one else knew how to deal with it, and they practically fought to convince me it must be my own fault. The more I planned things, the more went wrong — I could have been the spokeswoman for "Murphy's Law."

Having all but given up on my hope of a normal home life, I concentrated on becoming an animator. In desperate hope of having *something* go according to plan, I made the stereotypical journey to Hollywood — with twenty dollars in my pocket — to chase my dream. While trying to keep my head above water, I managed to meet some of the animators I had studied and admired. One of them happened to be interested in the spiritual and metaphysical, and being a Wiccan myself, we had a lot to talk about besides animation. He ended up "adopting" me as a protégé, and helped me when everyone else gave up as I struggled to adjust to life in Los Angeles and to my full share of serious problems.

My mentor, who was the only one who understood me, recognized that something was definitely askew, and reinforced my suspicion that it wasn't entirely my fault. He suggested we call John Livingston to see whether he could help, but just like 99 percent of the plans I'd ever made, something always sabotaged it. A simple phone call kept getting delayed for one stupid reason after another — for three months! After bringing up the subject late one night, we acted upon it immediately, making the call before anything else had a chance to prevent it.

I'd never met any psychics or had any readings done, let alone talked with an exorcist. I fully believe that unusual things can happen in what most refer to as the world of metaphysics, but I retain a healthy skepticism to balance that belief. I was prepared to politely tell John that while I appreciated his efforts to help, I really didn't think I was going to experience anything, but decided instead to give him the benefit of the doubt. I have to say I'm glad I did.

What intrigued me to begin with was John's pointing out things he couldn't have possibly known without someone having told him — he'd never even heard of me until my mentor called him, offered a few observations, and handed over the phone.

John performed an exorcism right over the phone. An entity or demon that I didn't know I had — but that "said" it had been with me seventeen years, since age four, left me, and I felt a very real chill go up my spine as it did. After John sent the being into the Light, he finished with a shamanic soul retrieval for me. The most incredible feelings came to me; parts were returned that I had long forgotten were lost, and when we finished I was so full of intense energy that I kept wringing my hands because I didn't know what to do with it.

The days after my healing were truly amazing. I actually felt *happy*, and couldn't explain why. My mentor assured me this was how most people felt most of the time, and that it was normal. I wasn't used to it, having lived most of my life with an attachment that successfully doused any scrap of goodness that came near me. The universe still threw me curve balls, though noticeably less often; they didn't turn my life upside down, and I was emotionally able to handle them. Good things started to happen, nearly as extreme as the bad that I had experienced before.

John had warned me that it would be a life-changing experience, there would be an adjustment period, and that it was ultimately for the better. My healing was reaffirmed by the reactions of people around me. Being close to me, my mentor noticed an instant change. People I worked with were again talking behind my back, but now the subject was how *alive* I suddenly appeared. The studio where I interned started trusting me with more work. I got four job offers in under a week, when it used to take me months just to begin filling out applications. I started making more friends. Great things would just *happen*, seemingly out of the blue. My back and neck, which my chiropractor had told me were those of someone twenty years older, became loose; I could be touched without pain shooting through me.

I won't pretend that everything is perfect now. I'm still adjusting to the incredible gift of having my life back. I was locked away for years, and have just been released into the sunlight again. I was at the end of my proverbial rope, and by some miracle of miracles, happened to meet up with someone who understood and had the insight to connect me with John. I believe my healing saved my life; I've been given a second chance, like coming back after a near-death experience. Life doesn't have to be the awful struggle it once was. I can breathe freely.

Heather Milne
November 2003

Acknowledgments

When I wrote the first draft of this book during 2001, most of the text was from personal experience with clients, and I am indebted and grateful to my clients for their teachings. Then I began to review literature and found that others had had experiences that supplemented mine, and from those I also learned. I give special thanks to Edith Fiore (*The Unquiet Dead*, 1987), who, through her pioneering book, taught me methods of hypnosis to use with possessing spirits, and William Baldwin (*Spirit Releasement Therapy*, 1995), for the teachings I gained from their writings about the invisible world of spirits and demons. I owe gratitude to my shamanic teachers, Michael Harner, Hank Wesselman, and Sandra Ingerman, for teaching me to travel to and within the world of Spirit to contact spirit teachers and helpers to "teach me what I need to know," and for teaching me core and advanced methods of shamanic healing that have enabled me to learn unique methods specific to my personal path. I thank Michael for removing the spirit entity from me and for opening the door and giving me a push. Many thanks are due Judy Lynn Taylor for her integrity as shamanic healer and medium during our years of partnership when I was first learning much of what is in this book. Thanks also to Joana Morris, Rae Milne, and Crystal Dawn Morris for their compassionate reading and comments on early drafts that led to this book; to the circle of Shaman5 for their loving support, and to Crystal Dawn for her shamanic midwife expertise that helped coax this book into life. I owe much to the editorial skills of Joe Shaw, of Cypress House. Any and all errors are mine alone.

John G. Livingston
Sedona, Arizona

Contents

Contents

Adversaries
Walk Among Us

Introduction

The Beginning

In private practice in 1977, I was counseling a young woman who claimed she was addicted to cocaine and had recently attempted suicide on two occasions. During our third session, she told me about all the relationships she had started with men, only to have them end suddenly. I was beginning to probe for a cause when instantly her attractive face contorted into a terrible grimace, and a deep, harsh, masculine-sounding voice came out saying, "Leave her alone. She's mine!" The hair stood erect on the back of my head and neck, and my forearms gave a jolt as if from an electric shock.

The dialog that started then seemed to go on forever, and whatever it was with, it wasn't the client's personality, which didn't re-emerge until near the end of the confrontation. When I said something like, "You have no business with her. Leave her," it would instantly find weaknesses in my knowledge of the supernatural and tell me in a growl that she was its whole business. And when I said, "She is no longer going to use cocaine; or going to kill herself, so you might as well leave her," it poked holes in all my guesses by mockingly telling me it could read her mind and I could not, and it knew her doubts and what she was

3

thinking. When I said, with seeming great insight, "You're not real, you're just my imagination and you can't really do anything," I felt a large, threatening movement toward me. Loudly, it told me it could control her actions in ways I couldn't even imagine — but I did begin to imagine.

But I began to make headway when I began to talk with it about my client's intent to give up cocaine, the changes she had been making in her life, and the dreams of the future she'd begun sharing. When I stayed with the things I knew, in contrast to things I believed, guessed, or bluffed at, I could sense its power somehow diminish. Then, with my encouragement, the client started talking, hesitantly at first, then stronger and stronger, as she sensed its lessening hold on her, telling the demon (for that's what it was), that it had to leave so she could live her life as she intended, so she could live her dream. I provided support, telling the demon its time with her was over because that was what she wanted, that she had greater purpose in life than to carry around a demon who desired only that she kill herself. The demon did leave — mostly, I'm sure, as a result of the woman finding her power to state with clear intent her desires for her life. And her dreams came true: within six months she had married a "soul mate," moved to a tropical island, and opened a restaurant whose fame I later heard about.

You might think that following this adventure, this initiation into the demonic, I became deeply committed, like one of Joseph Campbell's heroes, helping people rid themselves of demons. But that didn't happen, because, as I found much later, the demon that left her had transferred to me, a common occurrence for those without awareness, knowledge, and protection.

My life slowly spiraled downward into a chaos of doubt and

worry about everything, a general "falling apart" of the positive structure I'd built so laboriously. Within four years I had closed my therapy practice and reestablished a geology consulting business, which I continually tried to sabotage. Although I maintained a part-time counseling practice and did some depossession of spirit entities (using methods I'll describe later) I didn't see that as important. Several years later, both my parents died and I was divorced.

In spring 1994, in deep despair, I felt a growing sense that there must be more to life. In Sacramento I found a compassionate therapist who gently led me into a personal recovery program similar to what she, unbeknownst to me, had recently completed. Through a miracle of awakening, I stopping drinking in 1995. I closed my consulting business, and in spring 1996 went on an odyssey. During three months of travel and camping in the Southwest, I learned the meaning of the word "spiritual" and the miracles of being connected with the world of spirit. With renewed passion for life, I began an intense study of shamanic methods, and began seeing clients in a healing practice that included the removal of possessing spirits and demons. Since then, my life has been one of continuous change.

Why This Book

My theme is the removal, through ancient practices of depossession and exorcism, of parasitic demons and spirits. These spirits and demons, which attach to people's bodies to attempt some control over their minds and actions, are discarnate and invisible to our physical sight, but may be seen through the spiritual sight of the "third eye" by those with the gift. But why remove them? Because they have control, ranging from very slight to near total, over people's thoughts and actions, they drain personal energy, they impact people's health, and they drive some people to do terrible things to others, actions universally seen as evil.

Most of the systems we have created, such as government and our legal system, assume that we operate as individuals in a system of free will. Most believe we can freely choose what we're going to do, according to our personal values of right and wrong, good and bad, in each situation we encounter. But the legal system has modified those beliefs with certain other beliefs:

(1) That individuals experience periods of insanity, as diagnosed by a psychiatrist, when they are unable to know right from wrong in the choices they make; and

(2) Individuals (possibly acting as part of an army, country, corporation, or family) can be directed by the prevailing leadership (by brainwashing, threat to security or life, or appeal to patriotism) to make choices they know are morally or legally wrong. National and international laws have been modified at times to adjust for these beliefs, but at present, there are no legal adjustments to our understanding of human behavior with respect to the impact of invisible possessing spirits and demons on individual free will. Hopefully, this book will inspire legal experts to review the situation.

One purpose of this book is to illustrate how the possessing spirits and demons may interfere with or control the free-will expression of thought and action of as much as 75 percent of our population (Fiore, *The Unquiet Dead,* 1987). Based on the evidence of my clients, the percentage escalates rapidly at times of nationwide fear from the threat of war.

Another purpose of the book is to help people be unafraid of their personal dark side, that largely unknown part of themselves that is a repository of emotional impulses and urges that, if not afforded freedom of creative expression, are always threatening to explode. Also, to help people be unafraid of things that cannot be seen and are unknown, that are given names like "ghost," "boogeyman" and "spook." Myth, fantasy, lies, distortion, and lack of information surrounded unknowns. This book engages such unknowns as death, spirits of the dead, ghosts, demons, evil, and Satan. My intent throughout is to shine light on those subjects, removing them from the realm of shadow.

I'm aware that the subject matter of this book contains "hot" areas about which people hold sacred beliefs that they may have taken on as children and held without scrutiny ever since: the issues of God, Jesus, Satan, angels, archangels, demons, death, spirits, reincarnation, the dark forces, possession, and exorcism. I ask all readers, in fairness to themselves, to check such "baggage" at the door and read this book with an open heart. Allow in whatever resonates in your heart as truth; whatever doesn't feel right to you, let it go without judgment, so your heart remains free of clutter.

The greatest unknown or fear-producer appears to be death, which is one reason I discuss it. And a great cause of death is war, which is why the subject arouses so much fear. Another fear-producer is change. Death may be an ultimate form of change, but healing of life-challenging issues, primal wounds, and physical and emotional illness is also change, and requires the death of earlier ways of being. Anticipating this change brings about resistance and fear, as discussed by Carolyn Myss (*Why People Don't Heal and How They Can,* 1997). Beliefs about unknowns create fear, and fear, regardless of its source, creates stress in body and mind. And stress weakens the immune system, which leads to illness.

In my clients' lives, the removal of possessing spirits and demons greatly reduces fear and stress and increases their energy and sense of well-being. Symptoms such as tiredness, headache, nervous tension, inability to sleep, worry about lack of relationships and / or money, and feelings of being out of control, usually end when this root cause is removed.

Definitions

Possessing spirits or spirit entities (Chapters Five to Eight) are those invisible and discarnate human souls or soul fragments that have remained on Earth following death of the physical body, rather than ascending to the light, to Heaven, to the shamanic Upper World. To feel alive, and not lost and lonely, they attach with people, places, houses, and animals.

Demons (Chapters Nine to Eleven) are invisible, discarnate, non-human beings in league with the forces of darkness (Chapter Thirteen) with leadership from some largely unknown dark being(s) (Chapter Twelve), to create fear and chaos in the lives of people they possess. The giant demons and fallen angels attach with the people they see as threatening to the forces of darkness, wishing to steal their light, their soul, so they have insufficient power to fulfill their life's purpose. They are also chief components of those — whether serial killer or leaders of terrorist groups — who have traded their souls to the dark forces for power over others.

Depossession is the removal of possessing spirits and demons through:

1. Verbal dialog with the possessing being through a medium, or the client as medium, with or without the use of hypnosis;

8

2. Telling or commanding the possessing being to leave through reading a prepared script;
3. Praying that the possessed person be "delivered" of the possessing being; and
4. Shamanic journey and face-to-face meeting and dialog with the possessing being.

Depossession can be performed face to face or at a distance. Other authors and practitioners call similar practices "clearing," "spirit release," and "deliverance." Some practices are religious rituals, as in the case of "exorcisms" practiced by the Catholic Church since the third century, and the "deliverance ministry" of both the Protestant and Catholic Churches.

Exorcism, in the original and ancient form modeled for us by Jesus, is the removal of possessing spirit entities and demons through simple command backed by the spiritual authority and supernatural power of a being with power greater than the possessing beings'. Jesus' methods were quick and simple, and provided a return to health, as indicated by his exorcisms (Chapter Three).

Also, Chapter Three contains summaries of occurrences during Jesus' exorcisms that were invisible to the onlookers and his disciples, and thus were not reported, but left as mysteries in the stories of the Gospels of the New Testament; and of those that were visible and reported, but perhaps not appreciated by most readers of the Gospels.

By now it may be unclear to some readers, because of this talk of Jesus, whether these healing practices are spiritual or religious in nature. I'll share my beliefs in the form of a creation story. At the beginning of people on Earth there was intellectual darkness. Out of that darkness, in the many tribal cultures scattered over the Earth less than 50,000 years ago, within the minds of selected people (now known as shamans) within each tribe, healing methods were seeded as ideas, as spiritual gifts, from some beneficent spiritual being or power. The nature of the unknown, unseen spiritual beings and powers became known to the shamans as they learned to connect with spirit beings in other worlds and realities while in ecstatic states of altered consciousness. Those beings became the sources of tribal power and were described within the creation story of each tribe. The story usually described in some detail the cosmology of the spiritual worlds, which included supreme beings, lesser gods and goddesses, and elements and spirits. Some of these powers became known as benevolent and supportive of "good" life, a force of light. Others became known as adversarial and supportive of evil actions, a force of darkness causing catastrophe: pestilence, famine, and death. These dark beings are the subject of Chapter Thirteen, while the dark forces and the origin of evil are discussed in Chapter Fourteen.

In some tribal cultures, due to the belief of some who desired power over the tribe that they should be the intermediaries between the people and their gods and goddesses, these spiritual thoughts led to the formation of organized religious beliefs, rules and/or laws, and the organization of a priesthood to carry out the duties of the religion. Some did this to gain personal power; others saw it as service to the souls of their people. Usually, the tribal priests did not attempt to usurp or practice the spiritual healing methods of the shamans, unless they too were shamans. With variations among individual tribes, due to the varying degree of credibility and power given to each leg of a three-legged authority structure, elders or rulers maintained the physical balance within the tribe, priests maintained the religious balance, and the shamans maintained spiritual balance and harmony with the world.

The forces of darkness — those rebellious and invisible beings in a dimension near Earth that believed they could control Earth and its humans as their own domain in spite of the Creator God — attempted continually to gain control over the rulers and priests through temptations of power and wealth. Shamans maintained protection from the dark forces through their connection with their inner divine self (upper soul) and higher self (spirit), their immortal self connected directly with the Creator God. Though continually tempted to take up practices of sorcery, magic, or religion, shamans provided the core in the battle against disease, demons, and the dark forces. And so it has been.

Shamanism

Mircea Eliade, a French religious historian (*Shamanism: Archaic Techniques of Ecstasy*, 1974, 2nd Printing), did a review of world literature prior to the 1950s, being the first to distinguish shamanic from religious tribal practices. Also, he defined the shaman in a way that truly identified the "shamanic techniques of ecstasy":

…the shaman specializes in a trance during which his soul is believed to leave his body and ascend to the sky ["and meet the gods" – p. 509] or descend to the underworld ["and fight the demons, sickness, and death" – p. 509] (p. 5). (I have added brackets [ ] to clarify the subject and context of quoted material throughout this book.)

…the shaman is also a magician [performs miracles] and medicine man [performs cures]…he is psychopomp [guide for soul or spirit of the dead], and he may also be priest, mystic, and poet (p.4).

…a shaman differs from a "possessed" person, for example; the shaman controls his "spirits," in the sense that he, a human being, is able to communicate with the dead, "demons," and "nature spirits," without thereby becoming their instrument (p.6).

This battle of tribal shamans — against death, disease, sterility, disaster, demons, spirits of the dead, the world of darkness, and the powers of evil — has since the beginning gone on outside the purview of religion, and often outside the consciousness of prevailing religions, except that, since the first millennium, shamans and shamanism were persecuted by religions and governments in power well into the last millennium. In modern times, "urban" shamanic practitioners have taken up the "battle." Basic teachings have been provided us by:

1. Euro-Americans, such as Michael Harner (The Way of the Shaman, 1990), who created the Foundation for Shamanic Studies in the 1970s to teach core shamanism (common core healing methods extracted from tribal shamanism), and John Perkins (The World Is As You Dream It: Shamanic Teachings from the Amazon and Andes, 1994), who founded the Dream Change Coalition; and

2. Indigenous shamans of many cultures presently teaching around the world.

Jesus the Shaman

By using the definitions provided by Eliade, and reports of the words and actions of Jesus written in the Gospels, it is possible to state that in his actions, Jesus was, among his many capabilities, a shaman. He spoke and prayed to a higher power, whom he called "Father," in a "heavenly" world, for information and strength. He invoked that name as protection from an underworld spiritual enemy named "The Adversary." He went on solitary fasts and vision quests to deserts and mountains. He healed the people of his tribe. He exorcised demons and spirits of the dead, using a higher authority that he implied by riddle could be Beelzebub, ancient spirit leader of demons, or the spirit of God. He healed disease using command, the faith of the sick, his own saliva, laying on of his hands, and prayer. He raised the dead by calling back their souls. He sent "unclean spirits" where they needed to go. He performed alchemical miracles, transmuting of water to wine, and lack of food to abundance. He controlled the weather by command, and was provided sure footing on water. He taught the people methods of prayer, and about peace, compassion, forgiveness, and unconditional love, that were different from the prevailing teachings of the established urban Jewish sects of Pharisees and Sadducees. He may have been one of the Essene sect, passing on their customary teaching of "zealousness of the (Old Testament) Law."

In a country torn by rebellious wars, occupied by pagan Roman troops who held power of life and death, ruled by corrupt puppet kings, and ministered by corrupt priests, the people had separated from their connection with God, an action that Jesus set out to change. He provided a source of comfort, strength, and lessened fear to the common people who were ignored by the upper ruling and religious classes. He developed fame and a huge following among the lower classes, as well as jealousy and hate among the upper, by the healings and miracles he performed and the lessons of love he taught.

Jesus is still accessible today as a spirit teacher for any who choose, as are many other spirit teachers, spirit helpers, and guardian angels.

Spiritual Helpers

One such group of helpers consists of the archangels, who are messengers between God and humans, and their legions of helping angels. A simple request is all that is required for their help. The archangels Michael and Gabriel have taught me the nature and source of demons, ways to remove spirits of the dead and demons, and methods of psychopomp, guiding of the souls of the dead to where they need to go, to ensure that those souls leave Earth. The archangel Gabriel helps me with psychopomp by providing guiding angels and portals of light to the Upper and Lower Worlds. The archangel Michael helps me with exorcisms of demons by providing angelic beings and the Mighty Warriors of Light on Earth — special warrior angels who take demons where they need to go whenever I call. The archangel Lucifer, rather than being another form of Satan, as misinterpreted and taught by religions, has helped me to understand mysteries of the dark forces, evil, the dark beings, and the dark side of myself. Also, he has helped me close negative vortices that impact houses and their occupants. I call on the help of the archangel Raphael as a master of healing of the human energy body after the removal of spirits and demons. The powers of the archangel Uriel are essential for the containment of giant demons and fallen angels (Chapter Nine). Some shamans and practitioners may not recognize or work with the angelic realm, considering them to be inventions of religion, or spirit beings whose wings are "imagination." Angelic beings act as divine messengers from God, have authority for the creation of miracles, and are available to us as resources of teaching and healing. For me, born in Queen of the Angels Hospital, in the City of Angels (Los Angeles), to not work with the angels would be to ignore the divine synchronicities of my birth.

Shamans journey to gain new information from spirit helpers and teachers. Much of the information in this book has, as noted, come from my spirit teachers during shamanic journeys in answer to my questions. Information in shamanic journeys may be given literally, as if through lucid sight, or symbolically, in metaphor or mystic disguise similar to most dreams. The method depends on what material and at what level the teacher is teaching. Symbolic information may require insight and emotional detachment, the art of dispassionate viewing, for interpretation and clarity of understanding. I learned early on that anger over obscure responses to questions only made subsequent answers more obscure. My transcriptions of journeys, abbreviated or metaphoric though they may be, are faithful to the original information as it was provided.

Readers might be concerned about whether information obtained from a teacher in spirit form, during a journey in non-ordinary reality, is as valid as information obtained from a "real" teacher. Those concerns are natural and go back thousands of years. Immediately following Jesus' death and resurrection, as recorded in the "Gospel of Mary" (*The Complete Gospels*, Robert J. Miller, ed., 1994), Peter, one of Jesus' disciples, asked Mary Magdalene to tell the male disciples what she knew but they did not. She said, "I saw the Lord in a vision." (Mary 7:1). Then she recounted the information that she was given by Jesus, although four critical pages of manuscript are missing at that point. Following her discourse, Andrew said, "I for one don't believe that the Savior said these things because these opinions seem to be so different from his thoughts." Peter then said, "Has the Savior spoken secretly to a woman and not openly so that we would all hear? Surely he did not wish to indicate that she is more worthy than we are?" Then Mary wept and said, "Peter, my brother, what are you imagining about this? Do you think I've made all this up secretly by myself or that I am telling lies about the Savior?" (Mary 10:1–6).

My response to readers' concerns would be similar to Mary's: Do you think I'm making this all up or telling lies? Shamans from the beginning of time have brought information back from spirit sources for the community. Different shamans may receive different information about the same question from different spirit helpers, or even from the same helpers or teachers, but that is because the information is perfect both for the intended audience and the shaman seeking the information.

The Nature of the Book

The main purpose of this book is to provide methods for removing parasitic spirits and demons as a means of self-healing. Considerable background information is presented before that point so readers can understand the methods and consequences of a parasitic connection. The dark beings and dark forces are discussed so readers can have some understanding of a larger picture involving supernatural players fighting for control of Earth and humans in many dimensions and worlds.

The conclusion of the book is about the purposes of possession by spirits and demons. In a very small part, this answers why a Creator God would create or allow arenas of both light and dark, each with its attendant forces and "good guys" and "bad guys," for this world of physical consciousness. When we combine the direct information from Lucifer and Beelzebub about their God-given task of maintaining duality as a sharp contrast between light and dark and not allowing the boundaries to blur over time, we are provided greater understanding that contrast is the major force causing continual development of our souls.

The power of contrast between light and dark — which causes physical and spiritual pain — spurs us to make choices from our free will that more sharply define who we are. Most of us require many lifetimes and varied experiences with the forces and beings of darkness to consistently choose the path with heart, the path of light. Eventually, we can come to the realization that we don't need to wait for death; our path of light is leading each of us to a reconnection with our true self, our divine self, our higher self and God-self, while in physical life.

When I felt compelled to begin this book several years ago, I asked my spirit teacher what was important about writing a book, particularly since he had earlier explained to me that all essential personal learning is inward. He told me, "Exhort the readers to read, and to read with an open heart. Let the words go into the heart until certain words resonate to cause people to go inward and begin their search for their individual truth about who they are. They will not find that answer in this or any other book, only in their own inner journey. All of their answers are there. All of the knowledge required for their life is there. All of the teaching to meet any human need is there. This book, like all other books that contain spirit between the covers, is written to awaken readers to their inner self, to the longing and desires smoldering in their souls, awaiting the fanning of the embers by the excitement and joy of discovery." So, I urge you to read, have fun, enjoy life, be well, and dance your passion.

Chapter One

Demonic Possession Today

When a newspaper headline screams, "Family killed by husband," do people ever wonder how a family situation, with the implication that at some time those involved loved each other, could evolve to a point where murder would be the solution? And when another headline shouts, "Serial killer's sixth victim," do people ever wonder that these horrible tragedies have gone on since the beginning of time without change? Or do they think that it won't happen to them; there is no way they would be, not a victim, but a killer? Do people think at all, or are they numbed by the dancing lights of TV?

Daily items from the newspapers, television, or weekly news magazines offer examples, often in shocking living color, of the activities of people who terrorize, abuse, and kill others. At times, the victims and persecutors are unknown to each other, but many times there is blood or marriage relationship between them. Is there some contributing factor involved in these tragedies, something that turns love to rage and hate, something that causes people to do horrible and evil things to others?

In my experience there is one root cause for murder, torture, and sexual violence such as rape and pedophilia, and that is possession of the persecutor by a demon. Demons, agents of the dark forces, all of which will be discussed and explained later, drive the persecutor to the often fatal outcome through seductive manipulation of his actions and thoughts.

Are editors and publishers aware that many of their top attention-getting stories are examples of demonic possession? I doubt they would agree, or understand. However, stories can be examined from my perspective, to determine whether parasitic and possessing spirits and demons have played a role in the daily tragedies that play out among people.

I have assessed three of the major news stories of 2001–02 with the intent to review each and point out a possible root cause of the actions. The stories are the terrorist attack on the United States of September 11, 2001; the adjudged killing by a mother of her five children on June 20, 2001; and reported sexual abuse and pedophilia by some Catholic priests with altar boys (and girls) and seminarians.

Each of these stories is not unique, but is an icon for similar types of stories of demonic possession that go back to the beginning of history: fanatical attacks of revenge, killing of family members, and sexual abuse by those in power within an organization.

September 11, 2001

On the morning of September 11, 2001, nineteen foreign terrorists took control of four American jetliners. Two were piloted into the twin towers of the World Trade Center, New York City, totally destroying both those buildings, but not until most of the people had evacuated. A third was crashed into a section of the Pentagon Building in Washington, D.C. The fourth crashed into the ground in Pennsylvania, kept from a probable mission of destruction of the White House by courageous, determined passengers. In a short time, over 3,000 people died in the buildings and planes. This assessment is about the terrorists.

At least some of the nineteen knew they would die as a result of their task. What is the common thread that caused them to go on the mission of terror and certain death against this country? Religious beliefs? Belief in a cause? Desire for revenge? A fanatical leader who inspired and drove them to their end? Ignorance of what they were doing and possible consequences? Or none of the above?

Not having access to a living terrorist, I journeyed shamanically to my spirit teacher to find the root cause of terrorist activities. I was shown an example in my mind, similar to watching a movie, of a young boy growing up in a Middle-Eastern country. The components of his life, by the time he was a teen, were: fundamentalist beliefs in a religion that calls for killing to right "wrongs"; beliefs that certain other tribes and groups of people were natural enemies and perpetrators of ancient wrongs; beliefs that righting ancient tribal wrongs and the blaming of wrongdoers was a God-given right; a disbelief in forgiveness and a practice of "an eye for an eye"; limited education; personal involvement in warfare and other acts of terror during which relatives and / or friends were killed; a great fragmenting of his soul from the trauma of events of terror and war such that his aura was very dark and filled with large holes; possession by "demonic" spirits of people from his own tribe, filled with fanatical beliefs that tribal enemies should be killed in acts of revenge driven by the emotions of hate and fear; possession by demons to magnify the emotions within the possessing spirit and person to drive the person to do horrible actions; and ultimately becoming associated with a gang of like-minded persons led by a leader. In essence, these became father, mother, and family to the boy. His life was directed toward acts of vengeance to relieve the continuous obsessive beliefs and emotions driving him, and to gain love within the family.

The terrorists, through fanaticism ingrained from youth, coupled with personal trauma and tragedies throughout their lives in war-torn lands, are trained and able to project their terror and hate through violence onto targets pointed out by their leaders.

My spirit teacher showed me that terrorist leaders, having traded or lost their souls to the dark forces (see Chapter Thirteen), possibly over several lifetimes, in exchange for power over others, use hypnotic suggestion with their followers to highlight targets, to ignite outrage, to direct hate, to incite a desire for revenge, and to justify the righteousness of "God-mandated" murder.

My spirit teacher has shown me a typical "profile" of a terrorist leader. His inner teacher is a possessing "demonic" spirit entity, a spirit who in physical life we would call a "real bad guy." At the death of the bad guy, the spirit (actually the soul) did not go "to the light," but remained on Earth as an adversary of humanity, in support of the duality of the dark forces opposing the forces of light. At some earlier time it may have been the subject of a religious exorcism, where the spirit was removed from a possessed person, but was free to repeat the possession with another.

Typically, the leader is driven by a giant demon that controls him with the "voice of God" or the "voice of Satan." This being may have been present since childhood, as activator of the darkest of the imaginations and behaviors of the leader's personal dark side. It may have been the cause of brutal killing, torture, and rape. The demon's goal is to drive the possessed to the deepest inner depths of chaos and terror of which they are capable, steal their personal power (their soul), and destroy their humanity. The terrorist leader, and through him his followers (of both genders), obsessively carry out the willful demands of the voice, believing what they are doing is "right." But nearly every observer of a scene of their actions, as indicated by worldwide reaction to September 11, would call the outcome "wrong" or "bad" or "evil."

Andrea Yates, Mother

On the morning of June 20, 2001, news reports indicated that Andrea Yates, a thirty-seven-year-old mother of five children ranging in age from seven years to seven months, had drowned each of her children, then called Houston authorities and her husband. Her alleged statement to her husband at the time: "I finally did it"; and to the responding police officer, "I killed my kids."

In the subsequent trial, a history emerged of postpartum depression and suicidal thoughts and attempts beginning after birth of the fourth son in February, 1999; hearing voices and having visions involving a knife, including being fearful of hurting someone; being hospitalized in a private psychiatric hospital several times and being prescribed various anti-depressant and anti-psychotic drugs; and the death of her father in March 2001.

Defense attorney George Parnum mounted a defense of insanity, arguing that Yates did not appreciate the wrongness of her acts. Gerald Harris, a psychologist who reportedly examined her as to her mental competency, testified, "She believed that Satan was living in her, and that she and Satan both must be punished." The psychiatrist at the Harris County jail, Dr. Melissa Ferguson, also defense witness, testified that Yates told her, "I am Satan," and that she felt her children were tainted and doomed to suffer the fires of hell because their mother was evil. Psychiatrist Dr. Phillip Resnick testified for the defense that Mrs. Yates did not know the difference between right and wrong, that she was suffering from a combination of schizophrenia and other disorders including depression. Further, he said that Yates believed she was possessed by Satan and set herself up to be executed for the crime to thereby rid the earth of Satan (CNN.com / LawCenter). On March 12, 2002, Yates was found guilty of capital murder and later sentenced to life in prison.

Is Andrea Yates possessed? Are her statements of being Satan, being possessed by Satan, and of Satan living inside her evidence of possession? Did possessing spirits and demons command and drive her to kill her children? In my studies, whenever the name of Satan has been given as a reason for horrible or criminal actions, demonic possession was the most probable root cause.

What is criminal here is that she was given no help in response to her statements about possession prior to the death of her children; no depossession or exorcism of any attached parasitic beings was done. What is a shameful lack is that most of the psychotherapeutic and medical professions do not know about or believe in the human spirit or soul, or about demons and possession. Those of us that do know have been remiss in getting out the message.

Legal Issues

The following does not constitute legal advice in that I am not an attorney. However, it reflects my opinion based on knowledge and experience. If Andrea Yates was possessed before the events, was she following commands in her mind from what she believed to be Satan? In my opinion, based only on reviewing what has been published on the case, the answer is yes. And in killing her children, if her mind was demon-controlled, did she believe what she was doing was "right" — actions that a jury would later would find to be not insane but criminally wrong? In my opinion the answer is yes. And did she have free-will choice in her actions? In my opinion the answer is no. In my opinion the root cause is that she was driven by a giant demon that convinced her it was Satan and drove her to kill her children. And should she be found "not guilty" and set free if the above answers correctly state the situation; if it is shown that a demon with greater power than she controlled her mind and actions? My personal opinion is as follows.

Rather than a question of insanity, which does not get to the truth of such issues as whether or not free-will choice was available, I believe it should have been asked whether Andrea Yates was in control of her mental processes and physical actions at the time before and during the killing of her children. And how would that be determined?

The information is too well hidden from the conscious mind for legal interrogation to reach the truth. An interview and dialog with the possessing spirits and demons, using the voice of the client or a trained medium, monitored by video taping, to determine whether a clear understanding and subsequent legal decision could be formed about who and what was in control of the defendant's mind and actions, and for how long, would probably have served. But if it were determined that the defendant was not in control of mind and actions, that they were controlled by some parasitic being, then the legal system could well determine to treat the situation like that of those judged insane: confine them until, through psychotherapy and teaching, they demonstrate the ego "boundary" strength and ability to "practice right from wrong." And perhaps more importantly, that such a person, even with the presence of a possessing demon, would ask for informed help from others when an obsessing thought or an external presence would appear to be taking control of her mind and actions.

The "Sins" of Catholic Priests

During 2001 and the spring of 2002, people living in Seattle, Portland, Santa Rosa, Los Angeles, St. Louis, Cincinnati, Cleveland, Atlanta, Palm Beach, Philadelphia, New York, Bridgeport, and Boston had their news spiced with the latest sex scandal: Catholic priests brought to civil or criminal court by allegations of sexual abuse by former altar boys (and some girls) and seminarians. The numbers seem to indicate a potential for hundreds of priests, out of a total of tens of thousands in the United States, and probably thousands of incidents of sexual abuse, mostly since the 1960s. However, the epidemic is not restricted to the United States. During a similar period, cases of sexual abuse of minors have been alleged of Catholic priests in Wales, Ireland, Austria, Africa, Poland, France, and Mexico (BBC news).

As quoted in the press, Pope John Paul II passed his judgment about the issue at the time he called the American bishops to the

Vatican in April 2002: "The abuse which has caused this crisis is by every standard wrong and rightly considered a crime by society; it is also an appalling sin in the eyes of God." However, the Catholic Church views sexual offenses as sins to be confessed rather than as a sickness to be treated, a crime to be punished, or a mortal sin requiring excommunication. Therefore, priests in the past apparently have been able or allowed to make their confession, then continue in their parishes or be transferred to another diocese.

Phillip Jenkins (*Pedophiles and Priests: Anatomy of a Contemporary Crisis,* 2001) claims the situation is one of homosexuality among the priesthood rather than pedophilia (i.e., sexual desire for prepubescent children). He claims that the same situation occurs among the ministry of Protestant religions, although more heterosexual in nature, and that the cause is not the celibacy of the priesthood (regardless of how determined the media may be to show this as cause).

A different question has not been asked about the Catholic priests involved in sexual abuse of young boys, pubescent or not: are these situations of power, similar to male-female rape, where the desire is not for sex but for dominance and violation? Is the root cause one of possession, where possessing demons drive the priest to live out urges of their darkest dark side, despite conscience of "right and wrong," vows of celibacy, and "marriage" to the church, for the rewards of power over their students and followers? Do some hear a voice of "God," or of "Satan" ordering them to dominate, to violate, to create terror in their young subjects? Do some believe they are doing "right?" Affirmative answers would tend to indicate possession by demons.

But the unasked and unanswered questions leave us unknowing whether the Catholic priests have control over their minds, mental processes, and actions. If the root cause is "demonic possession," the answers would be a definite no. The mind, the thoughts within the mind, the obsessing of the mind over a particular desire, can be within the control of possessing demonic spirits and demons to the extent that the person cannot regain control of his own will and mind until after following an "ordered" action. Then he is allowed to rest, to feel guilty or ashamed or powerful, until the pressure begins to build again.

The World in General

The foregoing examples — mass killings, killing of children, and sexual abuse of children — are far from the ordinary situations of the evening news. They are so large as to cause changes in the world. And the people in the United States now have a more personal understanding of what terrorist attacks feel like, as most other countries do, and no longer feel invulnerable to foreign threats.

Each of the three situations contains the following elements that suggest demonic possession:

- Living a life of Jekyll and Hyde: terrorists awaiting their time within the normal citizenry of the United States; Andrea Yates driven for years to kill her children before doing so, but not being noticed; Catholic priests apparently obsessed with sexual abuse of young boys and girls, yet maintaining their other secular and social duties.

- Acting in an obsessed manner, unable to keep from doing some particular act: terrorists unable to change their mind from vengeance; the mother unable to not kill her children; the priests unable to resist sexual abuse.

- Hearing a voice, attributed to "God" or "Satan," or an

angel of God or of Satan, that directs them in their acts: although priests have not been reported to have indicated this to be true.

- Performing actions that are beyond or outside any of their mental controls of conscience, knowledge of right and wrong, religious or other vows, general cultural values, and criminal laws; actions that are felt to be justifiable, necessary, and "right."
- Resulting consequences usually are labeled as "evil" by other judgmental people, by news reporters, and by fundamentalist leaders of other forms of religion if religion is involved.

Demonic Possession

"Demonic possession" is a situation where a person's conscious ego mind, will power, and strength of character and resolve to do "right" in life are overpowered by the forces of possessing demons. If the person is blocked from his upper spiritual soul (see Chapter Five), or it has been stolen or traded for promises by the dark forces, he will be guided by repressed desires and emotional urges of his lower animal soul. Such humans have the capability of all the horrible and ugly things that one person can do to another to cause pain, terror, and death for purposes of the one gaining pleasure, sex, wealth from, or power over the other. At the darkest end of the spectrum exist terrorists, rapists, torturers, and murderers.

Since the 1700s and 1800s in the United States, homicidal acts that could by their strange and horrible nature be the result of demonic possession have mostly been prosecuted as murders. And the defense often has been one of insanity, requiring proof based on evidence from examining psychiatrists that the defendant did not know right from wrong at the time of the crime. There is no known crime or defense of demonic possession — but at times of the Inquisition and witch trials, there were.

People are no longer burned at the stake or hanged because of the trial-judged presence of supernatural and invisible spirits, demons, satans, or gods. The hysterical hunts for witches, the trials, and the hangings in 1692 Salem, Massachusetts, or the European Inquisition that resulted in the deaths of millions of innocent people such as Joan of Arc, may well have deterred the legal profession from seeking to define crimes or defenses that have paranormal or spiritual causes. For how could truth of the invisible be proven? What proof might be offered that a jury could know to be free of lies, religious hysteria, personal prejudice, personal vendetta, and fanciful stories such as happened in Salem and during the Inquisition? How else could a jury return a verdict of "Not guilty by reason of demonic possession" except with some long-needed revision of the legal codes?

"Ordinary" Possession

This book is based on my experiences with my clients and their possessing spirits and demons. My present clients are *not* like the preceding examples. They are not examples of "demonic possession." They do not have that degree of Dr. Jekyll-Mr. Hyde contrast or intensity of darkness in their lives. The major difference is that their souls have not been stolen by or traded to forces of darkness.

In other words, they are like you and me, mostly in their thirties and forties, with some in their teens, twenties and fifties, and rarely children or in their sixties. About half have families and half are single. About half have had some psychotherapy. Like most in this country, they carry emotional wounds due to some trauma at a very young age, usually before age five. Usually, the major wounding event has been discussed in therapy, in "support" groups, or with friends. But all too often the core of the wound, the personal belief about self and the major decision about life formed at the time of the wounding, is protected by denial, fear, or secrecy.

My client referrals are nearly all from other clients who say to a friend who is telling them about some problem, "Call John. He might be able to help you." The presenting issues tend to be lack of committed relationships, lack of money, lack of meaningful work, feeling separate and alone, depression, rage or anger, under- or overeating, and feeling abused. This may be similar to the clients of many therapists, but a difference is that no matter what method of self-help or psychotherapeutic help or medical help they try, nothing changes. The common denominator among clients who come to me nowadays is that they bring an attached demon and often three to four spirit entities that are souls or fragments of souls (discussed in Chapter Five) that did not go "to the light." The "light" is an environment of pure love, entered through a portal that illuminates the world of spirit consisting of many levels, called by shamans the Upper World, and heaven or paradise by religions. This world has been the subject of great esoteric teachings and mysteries.

Clients have complained that the "civilized" world offers little in the way of understanding or remedy of the parasitic entities and demons except tranquilizers or talk therapy. Talk therapy may heal the mind but does not speak to the spiritual soul or spirit, although since Jung's return to favor, the animal or shadow self has been given recognition. Tranquilizers prescribed for emotional therapy shut down urges and impulses and control behaviors, but also shut down creativity of the soul in order to produce "normality." And some medications mask the signal of pain, which is the physical sign from the soul that something is wrong and needs change, permanent change. If the person's life does not become different, there has been no change to the root cause. A common remark by many of my clients in the days and weeks following an exorcism is: "I feel very different; thanks for returning my life to me."

The New Spirituality

In the new spirituality now being created in the world, priests will not have to molest altar boys (and girls), because that will be in the collective memory of the "then" of priests. New priests will be able to choose that that is not who they are. Mothers and fathers will not have to kill their children, because the memory of those horrible actions by others in the past will be taught in parenting classes to keep the memory alive in new parents. They will be able to choose that that is not who they are. Budding terrorists will remember past terrorists in their family, village, or country, and will be able to create a different future by saying to the memory, "No, that is not who I am! I choose to be…" The choice of a state of being could be "love," "wisdom," "truth," "compassion," or "the way."

The following chapter recaps the history of possession and exorcism during ancient times prior to the days of Jesus. If you are pressed for time, or historical review is not your pleasure, I suggest skipping to Chapter Three, which addresses the practices of Jesus as a model for exorcism, or to Chapter Five, which concerns the process of human death.

Chapter Two

Ancient Exorcism

Written records cited on the following pages indicate that exorcism was practiced in the Holy Land and adjacent countries long before the time of Jesus. For those who have small interest in that history, which includes material from the Dead Sea Scrolls, I suggest skipping forward to the next chapter on the practices of Jesus, which form a model for this book, to liberate people from their possessing spirits and demons.

Exorcism 3000+ Years Ago

In the Old Testament, Saul, who was Israel's king at about 1000 B.C.E., was reported to be possessed (Scripture quotations from The Holy Bible: New Living Translations, 1996):

Now the Spirit of the Lord had left Saul, and the Lord sent a tormenting spirit that filled him with depression and fear. Some of Saul's servants suggested a remedy. "It is clear that a spirit from God is tormenting you," they said. "Let us find a good musician to play the harp for you whenever the tormenting spirit is bothering you. The harp music will quiet you and you will soon be well again." "All right,'" Saul said. "Find me someone who plays well and bring him here." One of the servants said to Saul, "The son of a man named Jesse is a talented harp player. He is brave and strong and has good judgment. He is also a fine-looking young man and the Lord is with him." (1 Sam. 16:14–16.)

The servants were sent out and brought back David, who became an armor bearer for Saul until the king was troubled by the possession:

> And whenever the tormenting spirit from God troubled Saul, David would play the harp. Then Saul would feel better, and the tormenting spirit would go away. (1 Sam. 16:23.)

Later, Saul again was possessed, and threw a javelin at David in an attempt to kill him (1 Sam. 18: 10–11). Then, even later, following a war with the Philistines during which Saul assumed the young David would be killed but was not, Saul again was possessed by the evil spirit and attempted to kill David while he was playing his harp (1 Sam. 19:9–10). Some time later, following Saul's death, David became king of Israel.

Solomon followed David as king and ruled Israel for forty years from 967 B.C.E. Solomon's abilities as an exorcist were described by Josephus, a captured Jew who wrote as a historian for the Romans during the six years of war (66–73 B.C.E.) with the Judeans shortly after the time of Jesus (*Antiquities of the Jews*, Book 8.2.5). Although the source of his information was not given, it was probably from stories passed down in the oral tradition that were not written and included in the Bible:

God also enabled him to learn that skill which expels demons, which is a science useful and sanative to men. He composed such incantations also by which diseases are alleviated. And he left behind him the manner of using exorcisms by which they drive away demons so that they never return; and this method of cure is of great force unto this day: for I have seen a certain man of my own country, whose name was Eleazar, curing people that were demoniacal in the presence of Vespasian [Roman emperor, 69–79 C.E.]. ... The manner of the cure was this: he put a ring that had a root of one of those sorts mentioned by Solomon, to the nostrils of the demoniac, after which he drew out the demon through his nostrils; and when the man fell down immediately, he adjured the demon to return unto him no more, still making mention of Solomon, and reciting the incantations which he composed.

Josephus later again described use of the root, named *Baaras*, as a remedy for possession (*Jewish Wars*, Book 7.6.3):

It is only valuable on account of one virtue it hath, that if it be only brought to sick persons, it quickly drives away those called demons, which are no other than the spirits of the wicked that enter the living and kill them unless they can obtain some help against them.

To my knowledge, nothing further is known about the root; whether it is available and still used is unknown.

Exorcism 2400 Years Ago

Oesterreich, a German philosopher and religious historian, undertook a review of worldwide literature on possession. His book, *Possession: Demoniacal and Other*, was published in Germany in 1921 and in the United States in 1966. Although a masterful compendium of case histories of possession, it is a minefield of racial and cultural prejudices. A self-proclaimed expert in psychology, he did not believe in possession by spirits but believed it was a result of "divided personality" (p. 45), "parasitic psychic obsession" (p. 65), "autosuggestion resulting from distress of mind" (p. 91), belief in the devil (p. 121), and "infection" from observing others who are possessed, not because of the demons, but from a "concomitant lively belief in the demoniacal character of their state and its contagious nature" (p. 92). He stated his prejudicial belief "that possession springs from belief in the devil joined to auto- and hetero-suggestion accounts for the fact that it has always been most extensive in the least educated classes of society." In addition to education and social class, he expressed prejudice against Jews (p. 171), although married to a Jewish woman, and toward the "primitive" races.

Due to the voluminous exorcisms described on clay tablets, Oesterreich wrote, "In the civilizations of antiquity, the country best known for faith in spirits and demons is the region of the Euphrates and Tigris" [rivers of ancient Sumeria and present-day Iraq]. He went on to say of ancient Babylonian writings that "up to the present they all have been concerned with the exorcism of sickness and not of possession in our sense of the word" (pp. 147, 148). Based on Christian literature including the New Testament, he said, "it appears that possession has been of very frequent occurrence in the Mediterranean basin since the time of Christ," not that possession was confined to the Jews, as "it was common throughout the world of late antiquity" (p. 159).

The earliest description of possession cited by Oesterreich was from an inscription on stone in a temple at Thebes, Egypt, attributed to the fourth century B.C.E., but describing an earlier occurrence. In this, the king of Egypt had taken as wife a woman of Mesopotamia (Syria). A prince of that country, father of the king's wife, came to him with a story about her younger sister, saying, "an evil has entered into her substance." The king ordered a "doctor of mysteries" to her country to examine her. When he arrived, "he found Biut-Reschid obsessed by a spirit; but he recognized himself [powerless to drive it out]." The prince again petitioned the king [each journey from Mesopotamia to Egypt took a year and five months]. The king then sent his counselor of Thebes, who had been given "divine virtue" by a god implored by the king, such that he became a god. Upon reaching her land, "then came the god to the abode of Biut-Reschid; having communicated his virtue to her, she was instantly relieved." The spirit that was within her said, "I am thy slave. I will return to the gods from whence I came." Later, according to the text, it did (pp. 149–51).

Oesterreich felt that the number of exorcisms found written on clay tablets in Mesopotamia and Babylon, built upon the ruins of ancient Sumeria and watered into lushness that may have formed the Garden of Eden between the Tigris and Euphrates, was proof that "as in primitive societies, all forms of sickness, including psychic ones, were considered as the work of evil spirits, a sort of possession."

Oesterreich found no evidence of "demoniacal manifestations" in the classical Greece of Homer and Plato. He stated, "In the mysteries, oracles, and Dionysian cult it was everywhere the divine, and not the diabolic … that streamed into the soul of man" (p. 156). Later, however, "In the Hellenic period spirits began to come forth from every corner … the air is filled with a horde of demons, they besiege man and take possession of his inner life" (p. 157). Oesterreich believed that the close contact established by Alexander's conquest (336 B.C.E.) of the civilizations of Persia and the Tigris and Euphrates, "the very home of demonology," caused the spread of belief in demons into Greece and Rome (p. 158).

Of India, Oesterreich cited research into Sanskrit texts of ancient Hindu medicine on possession: "Children's ailments in particular were attributed to demoniacal influences … because the suddenness with which in children grave sicknesses succeeds perfect health could not be otherwise explained" (p. 172). For adults, "The worst forms of dementia are attributed to a demoniac influence and consequently classed as possession" (p. 173). The author went on to relate that the Atharva-Veda includes many types of exorcisms. One of the rites for those said to be possessed by demons is reproduced (p. 174):

1. Release for me, O Agni, this person here, who, bound and well-secured, loudly jabbers! Then shall he have due regard for thy share (of the offering), when he shall be free from madness!
2. [apparently to the possessed] Agni shall quiet down thy mind, if it has been disturbed! Cunningly do I prepare a remedy, that thou shalt be freed from madness.

Oesterreich reported that Buddha's mother, while pregnant with him in India, was described as having great healing powers, including that of exorcism:

Women and maidens, who happened to be afflicted by being possessed by demons, or by insanity, running about naked and covered with dust, regained their senses by the sight of Maya (p. 174).

Exorcism Reported in the Dead Sea Scrolls

The Dead Sea Scrolls were found among caves near Qumran, Israel, near the northwest end of the Dead Sea, from 1946 through the 1950s. One thousand or more original scrolls were guessed to have been preserved in pottery jars sealed with bituminous material. Jars fell apart or were broken and the contained scrolls subsequently decomposed and disintegrated into more than 15,000 fragments and partial scrolls. Controversy still exists as to who wrote and stored the scrolls. But all the religious researchers seem to agree that they were stored before 70 C.E., when the temple of Jerusalem and outlying communities, including Qumran, were destroyed by Roman Legions putting down a Jewish rebellion.

The Dead Sea Scrolls (Wise, Abegg, & Cook, 1996) provides new translations for many of the scrolls and fragments. According to the authors, the Book of Jubilees (found among the scrolls, but not included in their book or the Old Testament of the Bible) contains a story of how evil spirits came to remain on the land after "the flood," said to have been created by God to destroy evil spirits and demons (and mankind). However, the chief of the evil spirits, Mastemah, complained to God that he wouldn't be able to "execute the power of his will," so God compromised and allowed him to keep one-tenth of the evil spirits (Jub. 10:1–9; *Fallen Angels and the Origin of Evil,* 2000, pp. 485–86).

According to Zecharia Sitchin's detailed and unique archeo-logical accounts of Sumerian history (*The 12ᵗʰ Planet: Book One of the Earth Chronicles*, 1976), based on recent archeological finds in present Iraq, "the Flood" occurred about 13,000 years ago (rather than the 4350 years calculated from literal text of the Bible by Archbishop Ussher of Armagh in about 1650), occurring at the end of the great ice age that covered much of Europe and North America. Immediately following the great deluge, the Sumerian (and original) Noah, "a man of Shurup-pak" (p. 375), from whom the Jews may have derived their later biblical story, began agriculture and repopulation, leading to great expansion of civilization about 5,800 years ago in Lower Mesopotamia, 5,200 years ago in the Nile Valley of Egypt, and about 4,200 years ago in the Indus Valley of India.

The Israelites may have obtained many of their stories from the Sumerians and later Babylonians, from Abraham ("Father" of the tribes of the Jews), who was born in Ur of the Chaldees near Babylon, and from Babylonians during their later captivity in Babylon (587–538 B.C.E.). Some of these beliefs are preserved in their creation stories contained in Genesis. Many of those beliefs remain unchanged in the minds of not only Jewish and Christian people, but also atheistic people around the world who have heard the stories.

In "The War Scroll" (1QM, 4Q491–496 in *The Dead Sea Scrolls,* Wise, Abegg, and Cook, 1996), Belial, who sounds similar to Mastemah, the chief of the evil spirits cited above, is described as spirit leader of an army of dark angels and the Sons of Darkness, in final battle with the Sons of Light led by "the God of Israel." The Sons of Darkness were led by the Kittim, said by the authors of *The Dead Sea Scrolls* (p. 150) to be a coded name for the Romans, the "bad guys" of the Qumran scrolls.

Of course, both Mastemah and Belial sound similar to Satan, a Hebrew term for The Adversary, more archetype than person, who takes a more prominent place later in the New Testament. *The Dead Sea Scrolls* contain several incantations and exorcisms that were used to protect the Israelites against evil spirits of those forces of darkness.

"The Songs of the Sage for Protection Against Evil Spirits" (4Q510–511, from *The Dead Sea Scrolls*), contains incantations "to terrify the demons who were leading men astray." The authors used brackets [ ] to identify damaged text. The authors' words inside the brackets are educated guesses from partial smudges:

> And I, the Instructor, proclaim his glorious splendor so as to frighten and to te[rrify] all the spirits of the destroying angels, spirits of the bastards, demons, Lilith, howlers, and [desert dwellers …] and those which fall upon men without warning to lead them astray from a spirit of understanding and to make their hearts and their […] {I would guess "soul"} desolate during the present dominion of wickedness and predetermined time of humiliations for the sons of lig[ht], by the guilt of the ages of [those] smitten by iniquity — not for eternal destruction, [bu]t for an era of humiliation for transgression (p. 415).

Lilith has been reputed by many to have been Adam's first wife, who rejected him for his demand that she lie beneath him. She was called the night demon "who lays hold of men and women who sleep alone causing erotic dreams and nocturnal orgasms," in Sumerian, Babylonian, Assyrian, Canaanite, Persian, Hebrew, Arabic, and Teutonic mythology (*The Book of Lilith*, Barbara Black Koltuv, 1986). In a Sumerian terra cotta relief dated about 2000 B.C.E. she is shown as a winged "lady of the beasts" surrounded by animals.

"An Exorcism" (4Q560) from *The Dead Sea Scrolls* (1996) is an exorcism or a prayer of protection from demons and possession:

Col. 1 […] the midwife, the punishment of those who bear children, any evil visitant or d[emon …] […I adjure you, all who en]ter into the body: the male Wasting demon and the female Wasting demon […I adjure you by the name of the Lord, "He who re]moves iniquity and transgression" (Exod. 34:7), O Fever demon and Chills demon and Chest Pain demon […You are forbidden to disturb by night using dreams or by da]y during sleep, O male Shrine spirit and female Shrine spirit, O you demon who breach [walls … w]icked […] Col. 2 before h[im …] before him and […] And I, O spirit, adjure [you against …]I adjure you, O spirit, [that you …] On the earth, in the clouds […] (pp. 443–44).

"Songs To Disperse Demons" (11Q11) of *The Dead Sea Scrolls* (1996), are attributed to Solomon, to be sung or said as protection from demons. The following psalm called on the Lord [God] and angelic powers to confine demons forever:

Col. 3 Great is [… I] adjure [you …] and the great […] against [you …] the mighty [angel …] all the earth […] the heavens and […] May the Lord smite you [with a mighty blow] in order to destroy you […] and by His fierce wrath [may He send] against you a mighty angel […] which [… no] mercy for you, who […] against all these which [shall be sent forever] into the great abyss [… to] lowest Hades, and who [… there] you shall lie, and darkness ... Col. 4 ... and those possessed by [demons ...] those crushed [by Belial ... on Isra]el, peace [eternal ...] (p. 454).

The word "adjure" in the previous two exorcisms, or prayers, comes from Latin meaning "to swear to." It is possible that the Roman Catholic Church adapted this word to their definition of exorcisms, as will be discussed further in Chapter Four, from scrolls such as these.

The following is an incantation written by King David to be spoken against Resheph, an ancient deity whom the Israelites thought of as a demon (*The Dead Sea Scrolls,* 1996, a part of 11Q11 above). This appears to be loaded with scorn as a psychic protection given to people to be spoken or prayed against a demon of possession that attacked during dreams:

A Psalm of David, against [...] in the name of the Lor[d ...] against Resheph [...] he will come to you at ni[ght, and] you will say to him, Who are you? [Withdraw from] humanity and from the ho[ly] race! For your appearance is [nothing], and your horns are horns of sand. You are darkness, not light, [wicked]ness, not righteousness [...] the Lord [...] [in Had]es most deep, [enclosed in doors] of bronze [...] light and not [... never again to see] the sun that [shines on the] righteous [...] and then you shall say [...] the righteous to come [...] to do harm to him [... tr]uth from [... righ]teousness to [...] (p. 454).

All of the different exorcisms, incantations, spells, and psychic protection against demons and spirits found in fragments of text in the Dead Sea Scrolls seem to portray the high concern of the Israelites, probably similar to those of nearby countries of the Near and Middle East, for the danger of possession by demons, particularly during sleep and dreams.

The following chapter presents a summary history of Jesus' practices of exorcism for the people of Judea, to provide healing by driving out possessing spirits and demons. His methods, both seen and reported in the Gospels as well as unseen and possibly little understood, are proposed as a model for exorcism and exorcists today.

Chapter Three

Jesus the Exorcist

Jesus came to the Judean people of 2,000 years ago as a holy man, a messiah ("the Christ" in the Greek translation), meeting prophecies that were written in the Old Testament. In his public life, described by stories in the New Testament, he provided us many examples of his mastery as a shaman healer, exorcist, alchemist, teacher, and mystic holy man. Jesus' practice of "driving out" or "casting out" (Matt. 12:27–28) possessing spirits and demons from people was a unique and important part of his healing work. Though this fact is downplayed by religions today, his practice provides a model that is more applicable and effective than any in today's world.

Those who have heard or read of exorcism of demons and spirits probably have their information from the Gospels, or from movies such as *The Exorcist,* the latter representing Hollywood's spin on exorcism as practiced by the contemporary Catholic Church.

Jesus' early experiences and education are a mystery. A channeling by a man named Levi Dowling, first published in 1907 (*The Aquarian Gospel of Jesus the Christ,* 1964), provides an elaborate story of his training by, and his teaching of, Eastern gurus and sages. Only in the gospel of Luke is one story given of how Jesus, at age twelve, asked questions of and answered questions by Judean teachers in the temple of Jerusalem (Luke 2:41–47).

Jesus began his life's mission at age thirty (about 24 C.E.), but not without protest. When his mother asked him to perform a miracle by creating additional wine for a wedding feast, he implied that he was not ready to show his abilities, to begin outwardly walking his spiritual path. Reportedly, he retorted, "Woman, what is it with you and me? It's not my time yet" (John 2:4). But he did comply with her request, transforming water to good wine, thereby exposing his powers to his new disciples. This is the first we are shown his capability of miracles. One or three years later, depending on biblical interpretation, his public life ended physically on a cross in Jerusalem.

The Gospels are written records of the life of Jesus. The consensus among religious scholars it that the Gospel of Mark was written first, but not until after Jesus' death (*The Complete Gospels*, Robert J. Miller, ed., 1994); that Matthew and Luke were written somewhat later (70–80 C.E.), using Mark and another or other Gospels ("Q" document) as sources; and John was written even later (90 C.E.), from a different source than the other Gospels. Others believe that soon after Jesus' death the writings were transcribed from stories that were kept alive verbatim in the oral tradition. Alteration and destruction both by time and intent have been suggested for the original texts written in Aramaic and early copies in Greek.

Jesus' Exorcisms

Jesus performed exorcisms upon seven individuals; I reproduce them here as they are reported in the Gospels. Additionally, there are reports of several exorcisms upon large gatherings, but whether individually or by group is not clear. I have followed the sequence of exorcisms reported in Mark, except that the two exorcisms that are in Matthew and one in Luke, not in Mark, are inserted in the order where they appear to fit.

The translations of the Gospels are from *The Holy Bible: New Living Translation* (Tyndale, 1996). Slightly different from literal versions and the King James version, it is a paraphrasing to say as precisely as possible what the writers meant. Great expertise in Hebrew, Greek, and theology is required of the translators. I added the bracketed information within the quotations only for clarity, and have omitted verse numbers.

A Possessed Man at the Synagogue (1)

A man possessed by a demon was present [in the synagogue at Capernaum] and began shouting, "Why are you bothering us, Jesus of Nazareth — have you come to destroy us demons? I know who you are — the holy Son of God!" Jesus curtly commanded the demon to say no more and to come out of the man. At that the evil spirit screamed and convulsed the man violently and left him. Amazement gripped the audience and they began discussing what had happened. "What sort of new religion [doctrine, teaching] is this?" they asked excitedly. "Why, even evil spirits obey his orders!" (Mark 1:23–27; also Luke 4:33–35).

Exorcisms at Large Gatherings

By sunset the courtyard was filled with the sick and demon-possessed, brought to him for healing; and a huge crowd of people from all over the city of Capernaum gathered outside the door to watch. So Jesus healed great numbers of sick folk that evening and ordered many demons to come out of their victims. (But he refused to allow the demons to speak, because they knew who he was.) (Mark 1:32–34).

So he traveled throughout the province of Galilee, preaching in the synagogues and releasing many from the power of demons. (Mark 1:39; also Matt. 4:23–24, 8:16).

And whenever those possessed by demons caught sight of him they would fall down before him shrieking, "You are the Son of God!" (Mark 3:11; also in Luke 4:41).

A Possessed Man, Mute (2)

[At Capernaum] Leaving that place, Jesus met a man who couldn't speak because a demon was inside him. So Jesus cast out the demon, and instantly the man could talk. How the crowds marveled! "Never in all our lives have we seen anything like this," they exclaimed. But the Pharisees said, "The reason he can cast out demons is that he is demon-possessed himself--possessed by Satan [Beelzebub, by most versions], the demon king!" (Matt. 9:32–34; also in Luke 11:14–15).

A Possessed Man, Mute and Blind (3)

[Further at Capernaum] Then a demon-possessed man — he was both blind and unable to talk — was brought to Jesus, and

Jesus healed him so that he could both speak and see. The crowd was amazed. "Maybe Jesus is the Messiah!" they exclaimed. But when the Pharisees heard about the miracle they said, "He can cast out demons because he is Beelzebub, king of devils." Jesus knew their thoughts and replied, "A divided kingdom ends in ruin. A city or home divided against itself cannot stand. And if Satan is casting out Satan, he is fighting himself, and destroying his own kingdom. And if, as you claim, I am casting out demons by invoking the powers of Beelzebub, then what power do your own people use when they cast them out? Let them answer your accusation! But if I am casting out demons by the Spirit of God, then the Kingdom of God has arrived among you. One cannot rob Satan's kingdom without first binding Satan. Only then can his demons be cast out! Anyone who isn't helping me is harming me." (Matt. 12:22–24).

A Possessed Gerasene [Gadarene] (4)

[In the country of the Gerasenes] When they arrived at the other side of the lake a demon-possessed man ran out from a graveyard, just as Jesus was climbing from the boat. This man lived among the gravestones, and had such strength that whenever he was put into handcuffs and shackles — as he often was — he snapped the handcuffs from his wrists and smashed the shackles and walked away. No one was strong enough to control him. All day long and through the night he would wander among the tombs and in the wild hills, screaming and cutting himself with sharp pieces of stone. When Jesus was still far out on the water, the man had seen him and had run to meet him, and fell down before him. Then Jesus spoke to the demon within the man and said, "Come out, you evil spirit." It gave a terrible scream, shrieking, "What are you going to do to me,

Jesus, Son of the Most High God? For God's sake, don't torture me!" "What is your name?" Jesus asked, and the demon replied, "Legion, for there are many of us here within this man." Then the demons begged him again and again not to send them to some distant land. Now as it happened there was a huge herd of hogs rooting around on the hill above the lake. "Send us into those hogs," the demons begged. And Jesus gave them permission. Then the evil spirits came out of the man and entered the hogs, and the entire herd plunged down the steep hillside into the lake and drowned. (Mark 5:1-13; also in Matt. 8:28–32 and Luke 8:27–33).

Woman's Possessed Daughter, at a distance (5)

Then he left Galilee and went to the region of Tyre and Sidon, and tried to keep it a secret that he was there, but couldn't. For as usual the news of his arrival spread fast. Right away a woman came to him whose little girl was possessed by a demon. She had heard about Jesus and now she came and fell at his feet, and pled with him to release her child from the demon's control. (But she was Syrophoenician — a "despised Gentile!") Jesus told her, "First I should help my own family — the Jews. It isn't right to take the children's food and throw it to the dogs." She replied, "That's true, sir, but even the puppies under the table are given some scraps from the children's plates." "Good!" he said, "You have answered well — so well that I have healed your little girl. Go on home, for the demon has left her!" And when she arrived home, her little girl was lying quietly in bed, and the demon was gone. (Mark 7:24–30; also in Matthew 15:22–28).

Father's Possessed Mute Convulsive Boy (6)

[Near Caesarea Philippi] One of the men in the crowd spoke up and said, "Teacher, I brought my son for you to heal — he can't talk because he is possessed by a demon. And whenever the demon is in control of him it dashes him to the ground and makes him foam at the mouth and grind his teeth and become rigid. So I begged your disciples to cast out the demon, but they couldn't do it." Jesus said [to his disciples], "Oh, what tiny faith you have; how much longer must I be with you until you believe? How much longer must I be patient with you? Bring the boy to me." So they brought the boy, but when he saw Jesus the demon convulsed the child horribly, and he fell to the ground writhing and foaming at the mouth. "How long has he been this way?" Jesus asked the father. And he replied, "Since he was very small, and the demon often makes him fall into the fire or into water to kill him. Oh, have mercy on us and do something if you can." "If I can?" Jesus asked. "Anything is possible if you have faith." The father instantly replied, "I do have faith; oh, help me to have more!" When Jesus saw the crowd was growing he rebuked the demon. "O demon of deafness and dumbness," he said, "I command you to come out of this child and enter him no more!" Then the demon screamed terribly and convulsed the boy again and left him; and the boy lay there limp and motionless, to all appearance dead. A murmur ran through the crowd — "He is dead." But Jesus took him by the hand and helped him to his feet and he stood up and was all right! Afterwards, when Jesus was alone in the house with his disciples, they asked him, "Why couldn't we cast that demon out?" Jesus replied, "Cases like this require prayer." (Mark 9:17–29; also in Matt. 17:14–21, and Luke 9:38–43).

A Woman With A Spirit (7)

One Sabbath as he was teaching in the synagogue, he saw a seriously handicapped woman [who had "a spirit of infirmity" in most versions] who had been bent double for eighteen years and was unable to straighten herself. Calling her over to him Jesus said, "Woman, you are healed of your sickness!" He touched her, and instantly she could stand straight. How she praised and thanked God! (Luke 13:10–13).

Visible Practices and Results of Jesus' Exorcisms

The writers of the Gospels probably were not present at all the exorcisms Jesus performed. They might not have witnessed any of the exorcisms, but obtained their stories from various storytellers in the way of the oral tradition. Also, they might have added personal elements that were or were not part of the oral legend and possibly not part of what occurred. The following is a summary of what was reported of Jesus' exorcisms:

1. Jesus, by his exorcisms, provided healing and a return to health for individuals who were unable to speak (mute), unable to hear (deaf), unable to see (blind), convulsive, rheumatoid, and berserk or insane.
2. Jesus performed exorcisms on adults and children, both face to face and at a distance.
3. Jesus' exorcisms were reportedly at the verbal request of the possessed person, or the possessed person's parent, and the demands or "adjurations" of the possessing demon or spirit.
4. Jesus did not touch or in any way physically restrain the possessed person.
5. Jesus used brief commands in his exorcisms. There were

no threats to the spirits and demons, nor were there cries for help to a higher power.

6. Jesus used a command voice, not pleadings, exhortations, or adjurations (as the demons were said to have done).

7. Jesus' exorcisms required little time. His command voice received immediate response from the possessing spirits and demons.

8. Jesus performed the exorcisms alone, without assistance or support from his disciples or others.

9. Jesus performed the exorcisms in whatever conditions and circumstance were occurring when he met the possessed person, without ceremony or structure, and without any supporting tools, objects, or manuscripts.

10. Jesus did not state that the possessed people's faith had healed them, as he does for all other healings ("faith healings") of illnesses that he performed as reported in the New Testament.

11. In two of the exorcisms, the possessing spirits and demons spoke out using the possessed person's voice. Jesus commanded them to not speak.

12. Jesus appeared detached, without concern or remorse at the fate of the spirits or demons, even when it was possible (though unlikely) that large numbers were sent to their apparent destruction with the herd of pigs.

What the Onlookers Didn't See

Like many shamanic practices, what the onlookers saw of what occurred during a healing was only a fraction of the whole. Like most shamans, Jesus did not keep up a running discourse or teaching of all that was going on. He appeared focused on two other areas: healing the person, and choosing what examples to add to his legend of who he was. The following, most of which was not seen or understood by the onlookers, was told to me by my spirit teacher:

1. The spirits and demons were (are) invisible. With his spiritual vision, however, Jesus could see possessing spirits and demons attached to a person. Until later, this power was not available or known to his disciples.

2. Jesus understood how the possessing spirits and demons were the root cause of much of the emotional, mental, and physical illness and disability in his land, and how removal of their debilitating energies would result in health.

3. Jesus understood that possession of the mind and/or body of a person was not a healthy or rightful action by spirits and demons; that talking with spirits and demons was not required to determine whether to perform the exorcism or to promote the person's health.

4. Where the possessed person was unable to speak to Jesus for one reason or another, Jesus' psychic contact with the person's higher self provided permission for the healing work.

5. Jesus' command voice issued from his heart with the energy of the fourth chakra, that of love, rather than from the belly, the energy of the second chakra, of power over.

6. Jesus knew that the exorcised spirits and demons had different places to go, and would be taken there by angelic helpers following an exorcism.

7. Jesus understood the purpose of possessing spirits and demons in the possessed persons' lives.

8. Jesus used the power and assistance of the archangel Michael and his angelic beings to perform the exorcisms, especially the sword of truth and light to control the de-

mons and demonic spirits, to conduct psychopomp of the spirits of the dead, and to carry demons (where pigs were not available!) where they needed to go.

9. Jesus was in a state of continual spiritual contact with God, whom he called Abba or Father, in a state known to shamans as "merging" with the Holy Spirit, the spirit of God. Jesus "explained" the mystery process to his disciples as "prayer" (Mark 9:29).

10. Additional healing work was provided the previously possessed people by archangels "behind the scenes" to correct the effects of possession.

11. Baal (Baalzebul, Beelzebul, Beelzebub) was an ancient Semitic god of fertility, storms, and rain, apparently revered nearly equally with El or Jehovah, until the prophets (Jer. 19:4–5) indicated God's displeasure (The New Smith's Bible Dictionary, Smith, 1966). Jesus was aware that the exorcists of the high priests were using the name of Beelzebub for their spiritual authority. But Jesus, to place them in a bind within a riddle, equated Beelzebub with The Adversary [translated as Satan in all English versions], and implied that the Pharisees, by their split allegiance with Beelzebub and God, would bring their kingdom to ruin (which came true in about thirty years).

12. Jesus had no intention of teaching or healing gentiles or pagans such as the Phoenician woman's daughter, who was at a distance. Apparently, that was not his spiritual mission. However, she was so in tune with him that he could not refuse her.

Jesus as Model for Exorcist and Exorcism

The twenty-four points above are the seen and unseen practices of Jesus the shaman exorcist. In the possessed person, they produced increased health within a short time, without added harm or fear, thereby reducing trauma. Those practices are therefore proposed here as the model both for exorcism and exorcist. Any practices or ceremony in addition to those described above are not part of the model, and would require justification in terms of new or additional information about the nature of possession.

In this model, the exorcist is humane, even loving and compassionate, not judgmental toward the possessed person. The exorcist regards the possessed as one who has become entangled — for reasons outwardly unknown, but spiritually related to important free-will choices made earlier in life — with possessing spirits and demons that are impacting the person's emotional and physical health, such that they cannot find healing for their symptoms.

Differences of Matthew, Mark, and Luke

1. A confusing difference is that in most versions of the Bible the author of Mark uses "unclean spirit" in all the examples of possession, except with the daughter, where both "unclean spirit" and "demon" are reported; while Matthew and Luke usually use the word "demon" or "demon-possessed," except that in Luke, both "spirit" and "demon" are used for the convulsive mute boy, and "spirit" is used for the woman bent double. The origin of "evil spirit" would appear to be Hebrew (e.g., the Book of Enoch), while "demon" is of Greek origin.

2. Matthew reports one exorcism (12:22–24) of a mute and blind man that is unreported by the other Gospels. This is nearly identical to the exorcism of the mute man reported earlier in Matthew (9:32–34) and in Luke (11:14–15).
3. Luke reports one exorcism (13:11–13) of a woman unable to straighten up for eighteen years unreported by the others.

Additions to the Exorcisms

Each of the Gospel writers, and later religious scribes, apparently felt that the readers needed to be shown somehow why the possessing spirits and demons obeyed the commands of Jesus. Also, the process and stories of the miraculous healings of Jesus' exorcisms provided them a perfect forum to tell the world, which at that time had no other clue, the "good news" (Mark 1:1) of who Jesus was. The spirits and demons could not be seen (though in two cases their voices were heard), so as far as the people knew, they could not be questioned as to the truth. For two of the exorcisms, therefore, those of the initial man in the synagogue and the berserk Gerasene, Mark, Matthew, and Luke had the demons and spirits shout out that Jesus was the son of God. This amounted to a spiritual public-relations campaign, even though the written part apparently followed Jesus' physical death. However, we know from the example of the exorcism of Biut-Reschid (Chapter Two) that in their writings the early Egyptians also gave the possessing demon voice.

Jesus' Authority for Exorcism

The Pharisees, the learned sect of Jews who apparently used their position to create a life of power and wealth in the midst of Roman occupation, resented and feared Jesus' abilities and wisdom. Early on they set out to destroy him by showing that he received his authority to cast out demons from Beelzebub, the leader of demons (Matt. 12:24–28).

Jesus passed on his authority for "driving out" possessing demons and spirits to his original twelve disciples as recorded in Mark:

> And he called his twelve disciples together and sent them out two by two, with authority to cast out unclean spirits … and they cast out many demons, and healed many sick people, anointing them with olive oil. (Mark 6:7, 13; also Matt. 10:1, 8). In Luke, this was recorded as instructions to seventy-two disciples, who returned from their mission saying, "Lord, even the demons obey us when we use your name. (Luke 10:17.)

Following his death, resurrection, ascension (John 20:17), and return in the physical, Jesus passed on his power and authority to all who believe: "They will cast out demons in my name. …" (Mk. 16:17).

At least one other during Jesus' time was using his name as his authority for exorcism. As Mark records:

> John, one of his disciples, said to Jesus, "Teacher, we saw a man using your name to cast out demons; but we told him to stop because he isn't one of our group." "Don't stop him!" Jesus said. "No one who performs miracles in my name will soon be

able to speak evil of me. Anyone who is not against us is for us."
(Mark 9:38-40, also Luke 9:49-50.)

Jesus never answered the question of what authority he used
for exorcism, whether it was himself, God, or Beelzebub, the
leader of the demons, even during his trial, when his life was at
stake. This subject of authority will be discussed further.

The following chapter continues the history of exorcism
from the time following the death of Jesus to the present. Most
of the examples come from records of the Catholic Church, as
many records from early Christian sects were destroyed, lost,
or never recorded.

Chapter Four

Practices since Jesus

Paul was reported to have seen Jesus only in a vision some time after the crucifixion. Apparently, he was given authority through the visionary process to perform exorcism of possessing spirits and demons, as recorded in Acts (reportedly written by Luke):

> One day as we [Paul, Luke, Timothy, and Silas] were going down to the place of prayer, we met a demon-possessed slave girl. She was a fortune-teller who earned a lot of money for her masters. She followed along behind us shouting [I am told she was being cynical and sarcastic], "These men are servants of the Most High God and they have come to tell you how to be saved." This went on day after day until Paul got so exasperated that he turned and spoke to the demon within her. "I command you in the name of Jesus Christ to come out of her," he said. And instantly it left her. (Acts 16:16–18).

The Christians were not the only exorcists of the time. Farther north, in the world of the Greeks, only slightly later, Oester-reich quoted Greek writings of Lucian (born 125 C.E.) about the practices of a local exorcist who was operating from some definitely non-Jesus-like model:

> I should like to ask you then what you think of those who deliver demoniacs from their terrors and who publicly conjure phantoms. I need not recall to you the master of this art, the famous Syrian of Palestine, everyone already knows this remarkable man who in the case of people falling down at the sight of the moon, rolling their eyes and foaming at the mouth, calls on them to stand up and sends them back home whole and free from their infirmity, for which he charges a large sum each time. When he is with sick persons he asks them how the devil entered into them; the patient remains silent, but the devil replies, in Greek or a barbarian tongue, and says what he is, whence he comes, and how he has entered into the man's body; this is the moment chosen to conjure him to come forth; if he resists, the Syrian threatens him and finally drives him out (p. 6).

Oesterreich quoted from a German text (by Harnack) about second-century Greeks and the "new" religion of Christianity:

> The distinguishing trait of belief in demons in the second century consists first of all in the fact that it spreads from the obscure and lower strata of society to the upper ones, and even finds its way into literature ... and the power of the demon, hitherto considered as morally indifferent, is now conceived as evil. ... the extraordinary spread of belief in demons and the numerous outbursts of demoniacal affections must be attributed to the combined effects of the well-known facts that in imperial

times faith in the ancient religions was disappearing, the individual began to feel himself free and independent (p. 158).

The pre-Christian Hellenic Greeks considered the *daimon* to be the personal god-like inner being of a human, with a core aspect of destiny or "calling" that will not be denied (Hillman, *The Soul's Code*, 1996). This is equivalent to the personal demon within the human, the coyote jokester described by Eric Berne (*What Do You Say After You Say Hello?*, 1972) as the infant who "scatters his food on the floor with a merry glint, waiting to see what his parents will do" (p. 123), also the archetypal saboteur described by Carolyn Myss (*Sacred Contracts*, 2001), which, just as a person is about to succeed in life, pulls the rug out from under their feet. The *daimon* is entirely different from a possessing demon. To characterize the *daimon* as demonic, as did Hillman in his chapter of the bad seed, is to confuse the two types of demons, and to imply that "bad" or "evil" can live within the *daimon,* which can at most be open to the experience of possession by a demon in pursuit of a particular life calling or fulfilling a specific life contract.

It would appear that the concepts of "demons," "unclean spirits," "Satan," and "evil" were carried into the Greek and Roman worlds of the first century. Possibly this was by early disciples of Jesus, and the pagans and Jews who were converted to Christianity before Paul began his mission around the Mediterranean to Rome. Possibly, the demons and their acts of possession followed along with Christianity, with Paul, and other immigrants to Rome; or the beliefs and knowledge of the exorcists among them, about possessing demons and spirits, awoke the consciousness of the indigenous people to the pre-existing presence of demons and spirits.

I have experienced this with clients who were not conscious of attached demons and spirits, or the cause for various symptoms in their lives, until they were removed. Then they were able to recognize parasitic beings that were causing problems with others. A skeptic like Oesterreich might use this as further evidence for autosuggestion. However, in distance healing, many times the client does not know when the healing will occur, and does not hear the words of the healing, yet, removing the attached spirits and demons from a person removes the symptoms of possession, and change occurs.

Apparently, according to Oesterreich's research, an epidemic of possession spread throughout the whole Roman Empire before the second century (p. 160). He quotes Justin Martyr, a Platonist philosopher converted to Christianity, who lived 100–150 C.E., before there was a distinct body of exorcists:

> For numberless demoniacs throughout the whole world, and in your city (Rome)[,] many of our Christian men exorcising them in the name of Jesus Christ, who was crucified under Pontius Pilate, have healed and do heal, rendering helpless and driving the possessing devils out of the men, though they could not be cured by all the other exorcists and those who used incantations and drugs (p. 165).

Only slightly later, according to Oesterreich, during the time of Origen (182–252 C.E.), exorcism was a procedure of prayer and authoritative adjurations addressed to the demon "so simple that the simplest man was able to apply them" (p. 166). The demon was threatened with punishments but was not questioned or spoken to. Origen wrote that the force of the exorcism was in the use of the name of Jesus.

As indicated in the following paragraphs, by the start of the third century there was a change in exorcism, from the simple model provided by Jesus, which he gave "to all who believed," to the large book of exorcism of the Roman Catholic Church, requiring adjuration, considerable exhortation, and much prayer and time.

During his tenure, 252–261 C.E., Pope Cornelius wrote that there were in the Roman Church by that time fifty-two "exorcists, readers and door-keepers" ("Exorcist," *Catholic Encyclopedia*, 1999). In the early rite of the ordination for exorcist in the Roman Catholic Church, the bishop gave each new priest the book containing the formulae of exorcism. Exorcisms continued as a major religious function, and the rites finally were formalized by the Roman Catholic Church in 1614, after much prompting by Pope Paul V. The rite of exorcism, called the *Exorcism Manual*, although modified somewhat in 1999, remains the accepted one today.

The *Catholic Encyclopedia* (1999) defines "exorcism" as:

(1) The act of driving out, or warding off, demons, or evil spirits, from persons, places, or things, which are believed to be possessed or infested by them, or are liable to become victims or instruments of their malice;

(2) The means employed for this purpose, especially the solemn and authoritative adjuration of the demon, in the name of God, or any of the higher power in which he is subject.

As can be seen in the last sentence, the Roman Catholic Church, perhaps in the same quandary as the Pharisees questioning Jesus, leaves the option open for using a spiritual authority other than God. Did they know something they are not telling?

The manual warned exorcists that they were dealing with an ancient and astute adversary, strong and evil. Some of the many ritual formulas are up to forty pages long, possibly in the hope that quantity of words will provide the solution. Contrary to the movie *The Exorcist,* the formal rites of exorcism are usually carried out in a church, with witnesses, and sometimes in public. At the time of the Spanish Inquisition, the fact of possession was sufficient for a death sentence. In France during the 1500s thousands of spectators attended public rites of exorcism (*Possession,* p. 103).

"Adjure," as used in the definition of exorcism, is defined as (1) to command or enjoin solemnly, as under oath; (2) to appeal to earnestly (*Webster's II New College Dictionary,* 2001). The word does not seem to have the same feeling of impact as Jesus' commands (Chapter Three). "Command" is defined as (1) to give orders to; (2) to have authoritative control over. This is much more descriptive of the power of exorcism, and in a sense helps distinguish between exorcism and depossession.

Catholic exorcism is said to be backed by the authority of God and the Bible, while prayers in between the verses and rituals of exorcism are for the benefit of healing the possessed person. According to Oesterreich, exorcisms lasted days, weeks, months, and even years. One part of the exorcism is said to read, "I cast thee out, thou unclean spirit, along with the least encroachment of the wicked enemy, and every phantom, and diabolical legion. In the name of our Lord, Jesus Christ, depart and vanish from this creature of God." In 1999, the ritual of exorcism was revised, both to change some of the ancient wording and to stress a requirement for psychiatric examination of the prospect — not to determine the presence of a demon, because as yet that is not included in medical curricula, but to determine the presence of mental health conditions. But unless the demon chooses to disclose itself in the office, which is most unlikely, the psychiatrist's diagnostic manual does not indicate which of the many symptoms of the many mental health "diseases" and "conditions" could be due to possession (an external source acting internally) and which due purely to mental or emotional health situations (an internal source acting externally).

In my view, the Catholic version of exorcism from the third century has wandered far from the model that Jesus clearly provided. Their "finished" exorcism has a strong chance of putting the suffering and homeless spirit or outraged demon back out on the street, looking for another host, or looping back to the same person — or to the priest.

Middle Ages

Information about possession and exorcism in the Middle Ages of Europe, according to Oesterreich (p. 176), is sparse and mostly contained within the sixty-one volumes of the Catholic *Acta Sanctorum*, acts of the saints. Oesterreich states, "there is not one [volume] in which under the articles *energumeni* and *doemones* cases of possession are not recorded." But he downplays their likelihood of adding anything new to our understanding: "We find the same stories of cures, which are already known to us from the New Testament … constantly repeated in the biographies and legends of the saints with a wearisome sameness."

In Northern Africa, about 1492, Oesterreich (p. 186) cites a book written by Leo Africanus, a Catholic missionary visiting the Sudan, a mostly Muslim country:

There are in that country soothsayers of a kind called exorcists. It is believed that they have in the highest degree the power of curing the possessed, because they now and then succeed in doing so. If they do not succeed, however, they get out of the difficulty by saying that the spirit is unbelieving (disobedient) or that it is one of the heavenly spirits. … They describe certain characters on the hand or on the forehead of the possessed and perfume him with many odours. Then they conjure the spirit and ask him how and through what part of the body he came, who he is, and what is his name, after which they command him to come forth. [Italics mine.]

From the previous paragraph, the describing of "characters" on the hand or forehead is similar to modern Reiki practices, and the use of "odours" may have been a form of aromatherapy using essential oils.

Post-Renaissance

For exorcism in the times following the Middle Ages, Oesterreich (p. 188–189) abstracted the nineteenth-century investigative work of L. F. Calmeil, a German researcher into the "epidemics of possession" that occurred in Europe since the Renaissance. He reported twenty-seven epidemics of possession between 1491 and 1881. These were all over Europe, many at Catholic convents and monasteries, in Germany, France, Rome, Holland, Austria, Spain, Sweden, and Switzerland. The epidemic at the convent of the Little Ursulines in Loudun, France, from 1632 to 1638, is well documented and illustrates the dangers to the practitioner of exorcism as practiced by the Catholic Church. Cases of possession began at the convent, then spread to the nearby towns of Chinon, Nimes, and Avignon. Cardinal Mazarin of Avignon was reported to have "controlled" possession by not allowing it to be reported in the news.

Father Lactance, the first exorcist on the scene, expelled three demons from the prioress of Loudun. Then, "while he was about this work … was much harassed by these evil spirits, and lost in turn sight, memory, and consciousness; suffering from sickness, obsession of the mind and various other distresses." He raved in his "malady" until he died (p. 93). Father Tranquille, also of Loudun, and "the most illustrious of all the exorcists then remaining," died of possession in 1638. When extreme unction, a Catholic rite for the dying, was administered to him,

> … the demons … entered into the body of a good Father, a very excellent Friar [Father Lucas] who was there present, and have always possessed him since; whom they vexed at first with contortions and agitations very strange and violent, putting out of the tongue, and most frightful howlings; redoubling their rage again with every unction given to the sick man (p. 93).

He was carried away thrashing and kicking. It is probable that some of these possessed priests and nuns were locked in their rooms and lived out the remainder of their lives under the control of possessing demons.

Luther, in his Reformation opposition to the Catholic Church beginning in 1517, as described by Oesterreich (p. 186, 187), personally undertook exorcisms, but was said to have considered the Catholic exorcism a "display of which the devil is unworthy," and therefore he "worked with prayer and contempt." Apparently, Luther's point was that, when exorcisms were first introduced [by Jesus?], wonders (no longer needed) were necessary to confirm the Christian doctrine that God knows when the devil is to depart, so only prayers to God should be used, not commands.

During the Reformation, according to research by Esquirol, a famous French psychiatrist writing in the 1800s and cited by Oesterreich (p. 191), possession was often a matter of legal proceedings, where "the devil was summoned before a court of law and the possessed were condemned to be burnt upon a pile."

According to Oesterreich (p. 101), "the growth of exorcism came to an end at the time of the Counter-Reformation. This was due to the publication in 1614 … of the *Rituale Romanum*" [the book containing the *Manuale Exorcismorum*, Exorcism Manual]. Exorcisms within the Catholic Church were said to have slowed in the early 1700s, probably in reaction to the Inquisition, and during the 1900s, due to a requirement for substantial review and questioning of a possessed person by the Church hierarchy before a bishop would order an exorcism. Although this is said to be for the purpose of ensuring that the symptoms are of actual possession, it could also be due to a shortage of trained exorcists (possibly due to the incidence of possession of priests during previous centuries, or due to perceived dangers in the rites). The official stand is:

> … with the spread of Christianity and the disappearance of paganism, demonic power has been curtailed, and cases of obsession have become much rarer. It is only Catholic missionaries labouring in pagan lands, where Christianity is not yet dominant, who are likely to meet with fairly frequent cases of possession (*Catholic Encyclopedia*, 1999, "Exorcist").

But the instructions go on to hedge, "In Christian countries authentic cases of possession sometimes occur and every priest ... is liable to be called upon to perform his duty as exorcist."

Shamanic Cultures

Oesterreich concludes with uncertainty in discussing voluntary possession among "primitive peoples, so-called shamanism," that either this possession was rare in early America, or if the social history were "carefully explored" there would be much more proof of it (p. 197). Regarding possession among the "primitive" Americans, Oesterreich states, "it is very surprising that the literature on the North American Indians should contain nothing relating to possession" (p. 289). He questions whether possession really is less frequent among American "Red Indians" than among "primitives" in other parts of the world, but he concedes the possibility "that the structure of the personality is more solid amongst the American primitives" (p. 293). Oesterreich concludes, from work of the German ethnologist Adrian Jacobsen (1891): "It is only on the northwest coast of America that possession is known to me with certainty"(p. 290). However, what was being described was "voluntary" possession among shamanic societies, who were gaining spiritual power through connecting with helping spirits by wearing masks empowered by those spirits.

Methods of exorcism and depossession practiced by shamanic tribal cultures of Africa, Asia, Australia, the Pacific Islands, South and Central America, Mexico, extreme North America, northern Europe, northern Russia, and Siberia have not been reviewed here, due to their wide variations, possibly based on cultural differences and the diverse personalities and spirit helpers of individual shamans. Some review has been provided by Oester-reich, and by Eliade (*Shamanism: Archaic Techniques of Ecstasy*, 1974), from reports by ethnologists.

Protestant Religions

Protestant religions came into prominence between the 1600s and 1800s, but they seemed to promote the belief, thanks to the negative beliefs of Protestant founders such as Semler, Schlei-ermacher, and David Strauss (*Possession*, p. 192), that posses-sion was a mental disorder due to autosuggestion or hysteria. Therefore, possession and the attendant problems growing from this root, were avoided as a religious responsibility, and left as matters for the budding art forms of psychology and psychiatry, and medicine, with its Inquisition-like use of elec-troshock therapy.

During the early 1900s, Pentecostal churches began praying for the deliverance of church members from evil spirits. By the mid-1900s this ministerial work began to spread to other Protestant and Catholic churches to meet the spiritual needs of possessed (or oppressed and obsessed) members whose symp-toms could not be relieved by medical or psychotherapeutic means. In the mid-1900s, the Spiritualist Church developed in the United States as an offshoot Protestant religion then swept into Europe. A belief in spirits of the dead — therefore proof of spiritual life after death — and the ability to speak with them, were the attractive new aspects of the religion. Some depossession of spirit entities was, and is done, by Spiritualist ministers.

During the late 1970s, in the Brazilian Spiritist Church of Sao Paulo, as reported by Edith Fiore in *The Unquiet Dead* (1987), there were between 3,000 and 4,000 mediums treating 15,000 people per week from all over the world for possession. Some of these mediums, from personal knowledge, presently practice in the United States.

"Deliverance" is defined as the act of delivering, or the fact of being delivered. One definition of "deliver" is to set free; liberate; release (e.g., deliver us from evil). The ministerial process may have begun in some places as a prayer for an oppressed person. But during the 1950s through 1970s, with the appearance, to certain compassionate ministers, of the voice of a demon through the mouth of a person being prayed for at various places, the practice of deliverance developed into one of praying for or commanding the demons to leave their host. Some Protestants applauded the practice, and some turned away from it.

Informative and useful books on religious deliverance have been written by Maxwell Whyte (*Casting Out Demons*, 1973; *A Manual On Exorcism*, 1974), Francis MacNutt (*Deliverance From Evil Spirits: A Practical Manual*, 1995), and Doris Wagner (*how to cast out demons: a guide to the basics*, 2000). Although Wagner's book seems overly rigid, her points appear cogent for today's Protestant religions (pp. 24–26). She concludes that "the church" is disadvantaged (in comparison to Satan?) due to "cessationism" (disbelief in the supernatural, including miracles, praying for the sick, and casting out demons), poor teaching, no deliverance ministry, leaders needing deliverance, disbelief in the demonic, lack of spiritual warfare tools (to protect against Satanism, witchcraft, and Freemasonry), and unfinished deliverance. She lists the following clues for indicating possible demonic presence: no personal control of a particular problem, a sense of helplessness leading to hopelessness, something comes over the person ("like lights going off"), or a voice says to do something terrible (e.g., pedophilia, which she reports that deliverance workers agree is demonic in nature).

Modern Catholic Exorcism

Gabriele Amorth (*An Exorcist Tells His Story*, 1999), the "chief exorcist of Rome" appointed by the Vatican and who "in nine years ... have exorcised over thirty thousand people" (p. 169), states the fundamental stand of the Catholic Church regarding the practice of exorcism, the power of "casting out demons:"

> This power which Jesus granted to all who believed in him is still fully effective. It is a general power, based on prayer and faith. It can be exercised by individuals ... does not require special authorization. However, we [? and I] must make it clear that in this case we are talking about *prayers of deliverance*, not of exorcism. To increase the effectiveness of this Christ-given power and to guard the faithful from magicians and charlatans, the Church instituted a specific sacramental, exorcism. It can be administered exclusively by bishops and by those priests (therefore, *never by lay persons*) who have received specific and direct license to exorcise.... Many, both priests and lay people, claim to be exorcists when they are not. And many claim to perform exorcisms, while — at best — they simply intone prayers of deliverance and — at worst — they practice witchcraft (p. 43).

This recapitulation of organizational dogma dating back 1700 years is only another instance of Catholics receiving advice that creates guilt if they seek out help from others for their health. According to what people have told me, many Catholics and non-Catholics feel a sense of fear when they hear or read the words "exorcist" and "exorcism." Apparently, this is due to the energy of fear that has been loaded into those words since ancient times, usually by having been connected with the word "evil" by preachers, priests, religious authors, and news reporters, who maintain their audience through fear, ignorance, or titillation.

In truth, the only power that words have to trigger our emotions is the power that we give the words from our belief systems, augmented by fantasy. A few clients have told me that they had to overcome fears about the kind of work I do, and what I am called, before they could phone me for an appointment. Also, some have told me that what I am called kept them from phoning, even though they had a feeling that my work could benefit them.

The Catholic Church does not own or trademark the word or the practice of exorcism. It was given to all. *Webster's II New College Dictionary* (2001) defines "exorcise" as "(1) to expel (an evil spirit) by or as if by adjuration; and (2) to free from evil spirits." No reference is made to a bishop or priest. Canon law, in my limited religious view, has little effect outside the boundaries of the Vatican and the Catholic Church (even though most Protestant authors seem to avoid the word "exorcism" and call it "deliverance"). Also, the practice of exorcism went on before and after Jesus, among the Jews, Egyptians, Sumerians, Indians, Chinese, and very early Christians and other lay people. Certainly the practice of exorcism, as described earlier, went on long before the Catholic Church. The word is used in Acts 19:13. Part of my intent is to bring the words "exorcism" and "exorcist" into the light of more common usage.

Amorth (p. 32–35) presented, from his experiences, the seven activities that he has detected of Satan or demons against people. First is the *ordinary activity* of temptation, directed "against all men." The next six, listed below, he calls *extraordinary activity*:

- "External physical pain caused by Satan" to saints and many others who were beaten and flogged by demons. "This external form of persecution does not affect the soul; therefore with this type there has never been the need for an exorcism, only for prayers."
- Demonic possession: "Satan takes full possession of the body (not the soul)."
- Diabolical oppression: "There is no possession" and the symptoms are about poor health, and about lost possessions, jobs, and relationships.
- Diabolic obsession: sudden or ongoing attacks of obsessive thoughts from which the person is unable to free himself, may lead to desperation and attempts at suicide. May be taken as, or include, symptoms of mental illness.
- Diabolic infestation: Infestations of demons that affect houses, things, or animals.
- Diabolical subjugation: people who voluntarily submit to Satan.

From my experiences, each of these activities represents symptoms of possession by demons. Possibly, differing depths of attachment of the demon are expressed. The Catholic Church, however, would only provide a rite of exorcism for the second extraordinary activity, "demonic possession." "Oppression," in my experience, often includes physical harm called "accidents" (of which I believe there are none), such as a person falling from a ladder, driving off the road, or having something fall on his or her head. "Obsession" may also include mental-health problems, but I have found possessing demons or spirits at the root of the incessant thoughts and activities. "Infestation" can be due to demons or spirits attracted to a house by a previous occupant, particularly where murder may have occurred. To me, "subjugation" is symptomatic of the deepest, darkest form of demonic possession, indicating that the person has traded his soul to the dark forces for some promise of power over others.

Baldwin (*Spirit Releasement Therapy*, 1992), revealed that from 1970 to 1980 — during the height of *The Exorcist* — there were more than 600 formal exorcisms in the United States by the Catholic Church. That is slightly over one per week, which seems a token compared to the likely number of people in distress from symptoms of possessing spirits and demons.

Michael Cuneo, in his reporting on exorcism in America (*American Exorcism*, 2001), indicates that in the times of heightened awareness following *The Exorcist*, many Catholics desired exorcism but were unable to obtain it through formal channels. To fill the need, compassionate priests such as Malachi Martin (*Hostage To The Devil*, 1976), operating independently of the church, began offering clandestine exorcisms to the afflicted.

Two of these modern-day exorcisms were witnessed (or conducted with coaching from Malachi Martin, as quoted by Cuneo, p. 48) and described by M. Scott Peck (*People of the Lie*, 1983). Before the exorcisms, Peck wrote that he had, in fifteen years of psychiatric practice, never seen a case of possession, did not believe that possession existed, and believed that there was no Satan. Following the exorcisms, Peck remarked, "both were cases of Satanic possession. I now know that Satan is real. I have met it" (p. 183)

Of the two cases, Peck described one as "hypomanic and intermittently psychotic;" the other as "neurotically depressed but eminently sane" (pp. 189–90). In both, "secondary personalities" became apparent during psychotherapy that were, according to Peck, self-destructive and "evil," but did not respond to conventional treatment for multiple personality disorders. Therefore, after a year or more of therapy, exorcism was arranged. The list below includes the details I gleaned regarding the methods of exorcism used, as Peck recorded them.

However, I must preface the list with a disclaimer: each item in the list shows a lack of understanding of possession, of the nature of possessing spirits and demons, the client condition and needs, and what the basic requirements of an exorcism are. Each step, with the exception of No. 4, should be prefixed with *Do Not.* The following is from Peck (pp. 186–89):

- "Exorcism, as far as I know, is always conducted by a team of at least three or more. In a sense the team 'gangs up' on the patient." One exorcism required seven highly trained professionals to work (without payment) four days, twelve to sixteen hours a day. The other required nine men and women, who worked twelve to twenty hours a day for three days.
- "Exorcism sessions may last three, five, even ten or twelve hours – as long as the team feels is required to confront the issue."
- "The patient may be forcefully restrained during an exorcism session — and, indeed, frequently is — which is one of the reasons for the team approach." Later, Peck concedes that in "easier exorcisms the team may be needed only to restrain the patient" because in the more difficult exorcisms of his experience no one person could possess all the skills required.
- "Finally — and most important — the exorcism team, through prayer and ritual, invokes the power of God in the healing process."
- "Exorcism is seen by its practitioners in terms of spiritual warfare."
- "Because it not only condones but insists on the use of power, I consider exorcism to be a dangerous procedure."

- "During the procedure of exorcism patients forfeit a great deal of their freedom."

Whatever the "teams" did under the name of exorcism had nothing in common with the model offered by Jesus, or what I describe for self-removal in Chapter Eleven.

In my work, in contrast with that witnessed by Peck:

- I would not work with a team, except at specific times with a medium when engaging in dialog.
- I would not restrain a client, although I usually encapsulate a demon in an invisible bubble.
- I would not spend more than fifteen to twenty minutes in actual dialog with a spirit entity, and in my present way of practice that would be only with a former relative of the client; I would never spend more than a few minutes in dialog with a demon, and that only for a specific teaching purpose for the possessed person. As a statement of fact, I have not encountered a spirit entity or demon that was not removed in one session, and the process of depossession only rarely ("in the old days") lasted more than one hour; I have not had one return, although I have had clients who picked up new spirit entities or demons within a few days, due to opening the same personal doorway through which the originals had entered.
- This is never a contest of wills, or a competition of power over. It may be spiritual battle, but that is metaphorical rather than literal in nature. Holding fear, or preparing for warfare, during a session would surely result in activation of the "law of attraction" to bring opportunity for fear and warfare. Anyone who is possessed as a result of the practice of exorcism can be depossessed. Be careful, but not afraid.

- Regarding forfeiture of personal freedom, clients should give up nothing during a session. All powers of the ego for saying yes or no must remain fully present. Clients must be the age of majority or older, and personally competent, or have consent of a guardian. For children, the minimum requirement is consent of the mother (at least one of the parents or guardian). After age twelve to fourteen, I believe it helpful to have the understanding and consent of the child ("to remove negative energies around you").

The next chapter discusses the processes of dying and death to illustrate the formation of spirit entities. This is followed by chapters on the nature of spirit entities, the nature of possession, and methods of depossession of parasitic entities.

Chapter Five

Death Is the Beginning

Death is the great mystery, and in this culture there are many beliefs and myths of what happens at death:

- "That's the end. There's nothing more."
- "It's all unknown."
- "It probably hurts something awful."
- "You wait in your grave until Gabriel blows a horn. Then you're judged."
- "If you've been good you go to heaven; if you've been bad (meaning something different to each individual, family, and religion) you go to hell."
- "It's a painless and joyful transition and return home, to the world of spirit and God, where life and expansion of your immortal soul continues."

What do you believe? To a doctor, death occurs when the heart stops. To a shaman, death is more complex and does not occur until the life-force energy ceases to flow, and the spark of life, the spirit, and the immortal soul have left the body. There are worlds of difference in the knowledge held by the two "professions."

The Human Bodies: Subtle and Physical

Body	Nature of Each Energy Body
Spirit	Our higher self, our essence on the spiritual level, our God-self, our connection with Creator and collective unconscious, our superconscious mind.
Upper Soul	Our divine self, immortal soul, evolving soul, seat of intellect and higher emotions, center of intuition and Christ-consciousness, subconscious mind.
Persona	Our conscious self, thinking self, ego self, layer of continuous thinking, level of will power, conscious mind.
Lower Soul	Our shadow self, our animal self, mortal soul, seat of impulses, urges, and emotions. Hidden creativity.
Life-force Energy	Electromagnetic energy body that supports life, our vital essence, vitality, essential to function of physical body.
Etheric Body	Phantom body, the Double. Can bilocate. The model template within which the physical body grows.
Physical Body	Physical vehicle that carries all other bodies, slowest vibration. Responds to thoughts, beliefs, intentions.

In the previous table I summarized some ancient and esoteric teachings about the nature of the human being, known from 4,000-to 8,000-year-old Indian Vedic writings, following the work of Roy Mitchell (*The Exile of the Soul,* 1983, John Davenport, ed.). We are much more complex beings than is commonly known, even to science. We are made up of a number of subtle energy bodies that each interpenetrate and surround our physical body. Commonly these are known as the aura. From innermost, adjacent to the physical body, to outer, from most dense to lightest, from slowest to highest in vibrational frequency, they are etheric body, life force energy, lower soul, person or ego self, upper soul, and spirit. All are invisible to ordinary sight, but more and more they are being seen, photographed, and quantified. Names and descriptions have been given each of these energy bodies by the Hindu, Hebrew, Greek, Egyptian, Hawaiian, Chinese, and others.

My spirit teacher has told me that the spark of life dies at the moment of death, and our spirit body separates from within and around the physical body, just as at birth we separate from our mother's body. Invisibly, this immortal part of us, our essence, zips to the light of heaven, the Upper World, there to return to Source. Meanwhile, our immortal upper soul, our higher spiritual consciousness, which during life became integrated with spirit, slowly disengages from the lower physical soul and physical body. This may take several days. According to my teacher, the purpose of this withdrawal time is to provide an energetic presence so as to reduce the pain of loss suffered by loved ones during their most intense period of grieving. At the moment of death, consciousness and personality transfer to the upper soul.

The lower physical soul is our shadow self or soul, which during life formed of many "characters," many sub-personalities, that developed to varying degrees at various times during life, but were never totally "owned" or integrated by the individual (such as the child, the student, the bully, the wanderer, the spender, the sex addict, the hermit, the drunk, the tyrant, the mother or father, the victim). At death, this lower soul separates more slowly from the physical body as it begins to decompose. These archetypal fragments disintegrate and return to the collective unconscious. Some of the better-developed but not spiritually integrated sub-personalities become soul fragments (Sagan, *Entity Possession: Freeing the Energy Body of Negative Influences*, 1997) and remain on the physical plane. Sagan defines these as entities; because they are a form of discarnate being, he points out that they could also be called spirits. The rest fall apart into astral dust. Entities that have some etheric material attached are capable of attaching to the etheric layer of a human, adjacent to the boundary of the physical body, and parasitically tapping the flow of life-force energy to sustain their essence as possessing spirits.

The physical body's purpose is to provide a vehicle for spirit and soul throughout physical life; to perfectly respond without an agenda of its own to whichever are at the moment the most potent emotional thoughts, beliefs, and intentions of the conscious and subconscious minds. After death the physical body transforms back to the water and elements from which it was formed, and returns to Mother Earth, regardless of whether by burial or cremation. Sagan has indicated that in India, where cremation follows shortly after death, the purpose is to burn the fragments of the lower soul, thus cleansing the etheric body, which then is no longer available to sustain fragments of the lower soul. However, if cremation is done too soon after death, the upper soul may be troubled by an inability to remain near the body to provide a presence.

When our spiritual soul reaches the portal of light, loved ones who have gone before, and even animal friends, are there to greet us (Sylvia Browne, *Conversations With The Other Side*, 2002). We clearly realize that we are not alone as we may have felt during life on Earth; that we are deeply loved by all, regardless of the type of life we led. During an initial period of transition, we undergo a detailed replay of experiences of our physical life on Earth. This is not for judging whether we were "good" or "bad," but to allow us to clearly appreciate and understand how our life played out in Earth's reality compared with how we envisioned it before incarnation. There is no judgment because "the Judge," as an archetypal entity, is left at Earth to disintegrate with the lower soul.

We, in the form of our immortal upper soul, then go to places in the Upper World for healing, teaching, rest, and play, to return to a state of balance and grace after our earthly experiences. According to my spirit teacher, how long this takes, in a world where time is not linear as on Earth, depends on the depth and intensity of pain and suffering accumulated on Earth. Each soul has access to a variety of master teachers who are there to help us understand unresolved issues. In addition, we have our "soul family," with whom we can ask questions and share information. Teachings that we receive are mostly for the purpose of helping us become more deeply conscious of our principal way of life — this could be teacher, healer, leader, warrior, lover, adventurer, explorer, caretaker, peacemaker, etc. Later teachings might focus on our next life on Earth, or our next role in any "divine plan."

After the pain and suffering of physical life have been healed, we may begin planning for a new adventure on Earth, with a new set of variables (sex, race, nationality, income level, etc.). We probably contact various members of our soul family to obtain their agreement to play certain roles in the new life. After all, as life on Earth is lived at present, someone has to play the "bad guy" to be the source of major life challenges, and who better than a loving friend? They are the ones who played major roles in our past lives; the ones with whom we felt some instant connection at the moment we met them on Earth.

Each of us has choices of how we return to Earth to further our soul's life experiences and purpose. We can go in physical form, or go as a spirit to guide and advise another of our soul family. In whatever form we return, the overriding purpose is to expand our consciousness in the physical world — where the major challenge is negativity — for the further expansion of the consciousness of All That Is, with whom we are one.

Formation of Entities

I learned about the formation of sub-personalities in the physical portion of the soul by working with a particular client over several years. I found that each traumatic life experience produces a new sub-personality as a mental construct that is kept buried in the subconscious. Generally, they include what was perceived as a severe criticism or judgment from an authority figure who, in childhood, is usually parent or grandparent; in later life that role is taken by teachers, priests, spouses, employers, and police.

The following characters or sub-personalities were identified from formative events in his life:

Age	Traumatic Event	"Characters"
PB*	Harsh sex, drunk father	"I don't belong here"
1	Rage of father	"Bad boy" – fearful
3	Abandoned by mother	"Orphan" – alone
5	Yelled at by father	"Scaredy-cat"
8	Beaten by father	"Rebel" – angry
12	Made to change (schools)	"Lost boy" – alone
14	Sexual aggression	"Bad boy" – ashamed
16	Fight with father	"Rebel" – confused

* Pre-birth

Some of the major events in his life reinforced previous characters; others formed new ones. He also developed "good" characters during the same time: friend, student, lover, hard worker, father. But despite a college degree and employment advancement, none of those were as strong, as intense, as those developed due to trauma. He attempted to deny those he considered "bad," but they became part of his shadow self and lower animal soul.

At his eventual death, any of these that were not integrated with his higher self, but had sufficient development, whether perceived as "good" or "bad," could become entities floating around in the world, each with its own emotional agenda, urges, and desires.

An entity formed at death from fragmentation of the lower soul could be called a "soul fragment," "entity," "spirit," "spirit entity," "ghost," or "spook."

In a traumatic death, from automobile wreck, gunshot, etc., the upper soul may be blasted in shock and terror out of the body. The consciousness of the ego at the moment of death transfers to the upper soul and may be in a state of shock and confusion. There is no pain, but there may be some lack of understanding that the physical body has just died. I have been told by spirit entities of those who died in this way that the portal of light was not seen, and therefore not responded to. Undoubtedly, many of these were lower-soul fragments that were blasted free of the body, rather than intact upper souls, a distinction I did not understand at the time. Nevertheless, I believe that terror blinds the soul to anything happening after the instant of trauma. "Sight" can be returned to these entities following a healing release of fear-based emotions.

According to what I have learned during depossessions, many entities are stuck in a memory of the last moments of their life. The images and emotions of their death scene play over and over in an endless emotional loop. The more intense and fear-based the emotion, the more intensely they seem to be stuck in the loop. The final scene may have been one where an individual was tied to a stake with fire blossoming all around, and feelings of outrage or terror, such that afterward the spirit entity continuously emits those emotions. Or, the death scene may be one of suddenly being shot in the chest while filled with the panic and shock of war. Thereafter, that entity may continuously re-experience the emotion of shocked panic, like that shown in the first twenty blood-soaked minutes of the movie *Saving Private Ryan*, or the total chaos and nighttime terror of the Vietnam jungle firefight in the movie *Platoon*. Or, the scene of death may be one of feeling helpless, filled with confusion, while restricted to a bed by disease and drugs, but with the grieving awareness of two very small children who soon will be without the care of a parent. Following death, this entity may remain filled with emotions of grief and anxiety. Fear, which is, according to Marianne Williamson (*A Return to Love*, 1992) the absence of self love, is the greatest mind-clouding emotion of all, and the foundation for all other negative emotions.

Dying

We have many fearful beliefs around dying: one is that death is painful, another that death is final, the end of life, and another that we have no control over the timing or method of death. A favorite in many families is that one probably will die at the same age as their same-sex parent. Eric Berne demonstrated the prevalence of this belief with many case histories, some of which are described in *What Do You Say After You Say Hello?* (1972). And we keep such beliefs alive and pass them on as part of the family legacy. Most are untrue and help neither the dying person nor the loved ones, relations, and friends standing around the bedside. It is important to understand, as I have learned while performing depossessions and past-life regressions, that the soul experiences no pain at the death of the physical body. In traumatic death, the soul is out of the body, watching the scene unfold from a nearby higher place. Feelings of freedom and release occur, although these feelings may be masked by the emotions preceding death.

We choose the time and way of our death. Plans for death and potential times for "exit" are written in the life contract (Sylvia Browne, *Conversations With The Other Side*, 2002). A time is ultimately chosen when the soul feels it has accomplished its life purpose; death may be the culminating act of the life's purpose. The apparently quite different lives of Mother Theresa and Princess Diana ended synchronously in 1997, accompanied by a worldwide outpouring of love that provided a healing for us all.

Especially in the case of children, death may be the major function of the lifetime: the purpose may be to expand the consciousness of the parents, or the community, or to advance medical science, or because of a desire to experience death at a young age. Parents must understand that they do not have the overview, the spiritual view, to know the life purpose of their child, who came to them with its own purpose. So, although they may not understand their child's death, they can allow their consciousness to expand around that death, so the child's purposefulness is celebrated rather than shrouded by the parents' ongoing misery and feelings of victimhood.

As a person's death nears, it is time for loved ones, relations, and friends to begin a process of separation from the dying person, to allow them the opportunity to peacefully separate from physical life. Mostly, we do the opposite, and try to hold on to the dying person through our pleading, demands for miracles, and "heroic" medical measures, to deny death and the return to "home." We do these despite the wonderful teachings about dying and death by Elisabeth Kubler-Ross (*On Death and Dying*, 1969), and by the Foundation for Shamanic Studies (www.shamanicstudies.org).

Much of our grief, sadness, and anger about the person's dying originates from unmet needs, or fears of what will happen after the dying one is gone. Because of these emotions in the living, the dying — from awareness of and compassion for what the people around the deathbed are feeling — have been seen to hang on to life, keeping the life force flowing into their physical bodies beyond the time when they were ready to leave this physical Earth. While communicating with spirit entities during depossessions, I have been told that a decision to stay after death came because of fear that the living couldn't take care of themselves. We, the living, have the responsibility to the dying to assure them that we can indeed take care of ourselves, or, in the case of children, that we will be taken care of. We all need to prepare more fully for our death and the deaths of our loved ones, for it can happen at any time.

Psychic (energetic) cords of dependence between the living and the dying need to be removed or cut by a practitioner in a ritual of healing and separation, allowing the dying person to more smoothly release from the physical body and Earth. On several occasions, my removal of possessing spirit entities or demons and / or shamanic soul retrieval for a dying person has allowed them to make a smooth and peaceful transition within a few days.

Experiencing emotions such as fear, terror, rage, anger, hate, anguish, and blame, indicates that the dying are in the initial stages of dying, and may need assistance to work their way through the emotions so they can move on. However, in our culture, when a person is dying due to trauma by others, many see it as justifiable to blame those others. Even when the reason for dying is illness or "accident," blaming commonly goes on; I've heard bedside visitors encouraging the dying to place blame, but blaming, as an early stage of dying, needs to be ended as soon as possible. Unresolved fear, terror, rage, anger, hate, anguish, and self-pity can clog the conscious mind and thereby prevent the dying person from gaining access to their spiritual soul. For a dying person to reach the final stage, acceptance, following the earlier stages of denial, anger, bargaining, and depression

(*On Death and Dying*, 1969), while he or she is still alive, those around the bedside need to help the dying process flow, rather than become stuck at one favored stage. The dying person needs to come, or be allowed to come, to a point of quiet, where the chatter of the ego can die out, so the Christ consciousness and the God self of the immortal soul and spirit can be felt.

Those who become stuck in denial, anger, bargaining, or depression are in the past, or the future, as regards time, not in the now, and the now is the only "time" when thinking and understanding can occur. All great master teachers teach the same response to the last stages of dying: compassion, forgiveness, and love. Forgiving is not about condoning the actions of those responsible for a death. It is the compassionate understanding that most people who commit the actions that lead to death do not know any better (those who consciously choose to do these actions, because they have aligned themselves with the dark forces, are totally different and will be discussed briefly in Chapter Thirteen).

I foresee that, in a more advanced time and place, grief and tears from the heart will be replaced by songs and dances of joy at the transition of a loved one. We, the physically living, will know they are going "home." We will know that their time and way of death was part of their soul's life plan. Consciousness, rather than confusion, will prevail in the world.

Only those who, before death or during the process of dying, make some emotional choice to stay here are stuck as complete soul entities on Earth. After death, some wander lost and alone in a state of continual confusion and suffering. Others stay more or less attached to a specific place, a certain building, or a particular person.

Stuck on a Piece of Land

In my experience, most of the entities that have stayed with a piece of land are Native Americans who have feelings of sacredness or dedication to the land where they lived in their tribal community. Some declare themselves to be the "stewards of the land," and guard it in conjunction with the spirit of the land, watching over animals, trees, plants, water, rocks, and sacred tribal places. Some of these that I encountered were former tribal chiefs, and some were medicine men and women. In Nevada, I encountered small "bands" of spirits gathered in community around one of these leaders. Some were willing to be shown the way to the light, to rejoin their relations who had transitioned before, saying, "I am tired and ready to go." Others were equally content to stay with the land, despite being fully aware that their tribes and their ways of life were long gone from that area.

Other entities are known to stay around the cemeteries where their physical bodies lie buried, so they are included with those stuck with a piece of land. They cast an *umbra*, the shadow of the earthbound spook in esoteric teachings. Those who can show parts of their energetic self as some misty, etheric substance become known as ghosts, and become the substance of myth, legends, and scary tales to thrill the next generation. But this does little to relieve the pain and suffering of the ghosts.

Mines, tunnels, and places where cave-ins or avalanches have occurred also appear to be places where entities are stuck on the land. As we ate lunch one day near a mine opening in the eastern California desert, my friend, a shamanic medium, remarked that a miner was tugging at her shirt. As I talked to him through her, he related having been killed in a cave-in. He was tired of being alone, with no one to listen to his stories, was ready to be relieved of confusion, and willing to go to a world of light and love, so we delivered him to the light and went our way.

Every battlefield is a gathering place for many of the entities whose physical bodies died in that area. Death in battle usually entails terror and shock, the body sometimes blown into scattered parts, or disintegrated, as in atomic blasts. Physical (lower) soul fragments may remain trapped in the emotional loop of the time and event of their death. In places that have had many battles or wars over time — Israel, Iraq, Turkey, Greece, India, China, Germany, England, France, Mexico, New Mexico, and others — not only have many soul fragments collected on the land, but also in or under buildings constructed over the battlefields. The entities of warriors and soldiers that I have encountered during the clearing of houses and people (depossessions) may be mild and passive, or irritated and aggressive due to perceived encroachment. Some, known as poltergeists, which are ghosts throwing tantrums (Iris Belhayes, *Spirit Guides,* 1985), have sufficient willpower and command of energy to cause objects to move and people or animals to become hurt by what amounts to a curse by the entity.

Soldiers who are accepting of death, well trained for their task despite the fears that may arise, and who stay in the present without allowing their imaginations to create scenes of horror in some mythical future, are likely to survive impossible battle after battle, or go directly to the light following death.

Stuck in a Building

Many lost, confused, and suffering entities stay around the hospital where their physical bodies died during operations or due to illness. This adds their fear-based emotional content to the energetic spirit or feeling of the building, which often can be felt by healthy visitors as a palpable sensation. Sensitive and empathic people may have very strong reactions, including feeling anxious, fearful, and ill. A shamanic practitioner could easily "depossess" such entities from the building and grounds periodically, and sent them on to the light. A nurse who is a friend of mine has recently begun a daily ritual for moving on souls of the dead at her hospital. Also, a program of pain management — teaching self hypnosis and relaxation to patients who are dying in physical pain — would probably reduce prescription charges, increase the level of patient awareness and cooperation, and reduce the number of entities stuck on Earth. Dying people need to be taught that full consciousness, at least as much as possible, is more important to their soul's eternal life than the deadening of pain. However, until departed doctors report "scientific facts" back (from the Upper World) to living doctors, there will probably be little change to the currently escalating practices of pain control and drug usage.

Spirit entities, especially poltergeists, that stay as ghosts with a particular building are the most famous, or have had the most books and articles written about them for tourists. I have known some that rattle window shades, blow out candles, knock down pictures, open doors, and create odors and sounds such as footsteps. They usually have a deep emotional family connection with the house, and sometimes with one room in it. "Ghost-busting" of buildings, to remove spirit entities when they agree to be helped on to the light, can "relieve" a building of emotions of pain, suffering, fear, and anger that might be present from these discarnate beings. From personal experience with the depossession of houses, I know this relieves the anxiety of owners living in the house, and of real estate agents attempting to sell it.

Stuck with a Person

Many entities are stuck with people in a parasitic attachment called possession. The entity, whether soul fragment or complete soul, has chosen to merge with a human physical and energetic body to gain energy from that person's etheric layer, to gain the ability to see out through someone's eyes and thereby "have a life." In my experience, most times there is more than one possessing entity, often three or four, which adds exponentially to the complexity of voices, opinions, desires, and impulses within the possessed human's mind. In fact, possession literally means to possess the ability to influence and / or control a living person's mind, emotions, and actions. Each entity has its own degree of will and ability (power) to exert control over human minds and actions, to interfere with free will, and add to the impulses of the "dark side" of their human habitation.

The New Spirituality

In the new spirituality being created on Earth at this time, souls of those who die will be conscious of and prepared for life after death. They will be aware of their immortal soul, know of the world of heaven, and know that life is continuous. Fear of death will disappear. The transition from the physical world will be an occasion of celebration and joy.

The following two chapters explore the phenomena of possession. Chapter Six is a detailed discussion of those souls and soul fragments of human beings that remain on Earth following death, and Chapter Seven provides, from my experiences with clients, detailed information about possession by entities.

Chapter Six

What Are Spirits?

When we feel the essence of something, we are feeling its spirit. Although invisible, the presence of spirit is the indicator that something is alive. This is easy to understand with sentient beings such as humans, animals, and even trees, and insects, but what about a lake or a mountain? Yes, we can feel their essence, too, especially in the silence of the wilderness. Therefore they must be alive, as are a canyon, the ocean, the wind, and the rock that we pick up on a hike. Shamans know that all of these living beings have spirits, because they can journey to them and communicate with them.

But what about manmade structures — do buildings and highways have spirits? Every structure has an essence, a spirit, and is living, even though seemingly much different from humans. The spirit of a building can be felt just as can the spirit of a tree.

However, there are two categories of spirits that have more to do with my subject: the unenlightened and the benevolent. Benevolent spirits come from the shamanic Upper and Lower Worlds to help those on Earth as guides, teachers, healers, helpers, guardian angels, and angels. They may remain invisible, or may manifest in the physical to help a specific person, as was portrayed by John Travolta in the movie *Michael*, Brad Pitt in *Meet Joe Black*, and Will Smith in *The Legend of Bagger Vance*. Throughout much of the world, workshops are held to teach people the shamanic journey so they can meet and communicate with spirit teachers and helpers. Spirits provide help from the compassion and unconditional love they hold for humans. Many of them have been incarnate here on Earth and personally know the pain and suffering we experience in this world of negativity and weighty gravity. These benevolent spirits speak only the truth with us and will do us no harm. They do not interfere with our choices in life, but will advise us freely when we ask for help.

The unenlightened ones, the chief subject of this part of the book, are those stuck on Earth as intact souls due to choices they made while living, or as fragments of souls from the disintegration of the lower physical soul at death.

There is a small but spiritually very important third group of souls, usually of indigenous peoples, who have chosen to stay following death to be "stewards of the land" for the protection and care of their people and the Earth.

Unenlightened spirits are the souls that remain stuck on Earth by choice. In cases of revenge and unfinished business, that choice, that intention, is usually made during the death scene in the time shortly before death, but is sometimes made earlier in life. Those who died in terror and shock, or in a state of drugged confusion (drugs, alcohol, anesthetics), are stuck here because they did not see the portal of light at the time of their death, yet others with seemingly similar deaths go on to the light.

Some or most of these spirit entities on Earth are fragments of souls. They resulted from the natural fragmentation of the lower physical soul following death, not from some choice of

the conscious or subconscious mind to stay. Those soul fragments, entities, are usually more one-dimensional than an intact
soul, with a singular focus such as outrage, sadness, or confusion
about death.

I have encountered a number of reasons why spirit entities
remain on Earth after the death of their physical body:

Revenge

This group includes those who died holding powerful emotions
of rage or hatred fueled by an intense desire to get even with
those whom they blame for their death. During depossessions,
many of these entities report histories of having died by fire
and torture during the Inquisition or other times of spiritual
prejudice. All in my experience have been male (which is not
to say that all are males).

According to their stories, some of this group lived as peaceful
healers administering herbs and potions within their communities. Others were mystics teaching alternative spiritual practices.
Not all lived such positive lives of service, however; a number
reported having been sorcerers, practicing black arts to control
other humans, and spirit entities, for their own purposes. An
example was related to me by the entity of a very angry young
man who protested that he had been killed at age twenty-five
in 1600s England for practicing sorcery. He vowed to get even
with those who had judged him, and because of this free-will
choice he was stuck on Earth after death. Because he would
suddenly break into anger for no apparent reason, a client came
to me with, as it turned out, this entity attached. He felt there
was someone "with him." During depossession, the entity could
not at first remember his name, age, or why he had died. After

I had induced a relaxed state of hypnotic trance, he was able to remember his death, but kept trying to redirect the conversation to the justification for his anger at the injustice of the judgment against him — trying, in other words, to deny the scene and realization of his death. Eventually, with gentle but unyielding coaxing toward his truth, he was able to watch his life from the moment of being judged until his death. While his body was burning, he was watching from a distance and somewhat above, entirely without pain, but totally aware of his anger at what had been done to him. At the suggestion to empty all emotions, his face (as expressed through the client's face), earlier rigid with anger, slowly metamorphosed into one of softness, like wax around the rim of a burning candle. Then he was able to talk unemotionally and truthfully of his black sorcery practices that had led to his death. And then he was ready to leave Earth and go home to the light. The client remarked on a feeling of peace, and feeling strange without his usual tension and anger.

Several of the more verbally violent of those seeking revenge told me of having been the subject of religious exorcisms in which where they were called "devil" or "demon" during the ritual. Mention of the word "God" was sufficient to ignite anger against a concept they hated. In an attempt to live up to their priest-given names, some bragged of having been the cause of human death after their own deaths. I term these spirit entities "demonic," but they are completely different from the demons described in Chapter Nine. They were extremely fearful that going to the light was a trap that would take them to hell for their actions. They needed to be told emphatically that there is no such place as hell in any level of any known world; that the concept of hell is an invention of religion to keep people in fear; and that the only hell known is that of a horribly tormenting, negative emotional life while on Earth (though it appears possible that anyone convinced that he deserves hell can create that environment following death).

Terror and Shock

People die in the midst of war, catastrophes, and accidents. Terror in war is understandable. Through a shamanic medium, the entity of one Native American told me about being shot in the chest by U.S. Cavalry during the Modoc Indian war in northern California, and being in such a state of terror at the impact (not pain) that his soul flew out of his body and took refuge in a lava tunnel, where he stayed in deep fear for more than one hundred years.

Not all men who die in battle die in terror. During past-life regression to the death scenes of clients who have been warriors, those who stayed focused on their immediate tasks, "stayed in the now," and functioned effectively from training, went on to the light even though killed in battle. Those who remained appear to have become stuck in the emotion of terror, stuck in fears of some mythical future, and were unable to be in the present moment.

Many of the catastrophes reported by entities stuck here were caused naturally: landslides, rock falls, cave-ins, and earthquakes with building collapse. Accidents, although in my experience there are no accidents, were invariably in vehicles, airplanes, or motorcycles. One aspect of terror appears to be a soul's refusal or inability to leave the place of death. However, the following event is contrary to that fact.

On September 11, 2001, four U.S. jetliners were taken over and piloted by terrorists, two into the twin towers of the

World Trade Center, destroying them, one into the Pentagon, and one into the earth of Pennsylvania, causing the deaths of more than 3,000 people. In the weeks following this horrific event, I and other shamans worldwide, practicing psychopomp, helped souls of the dead leave the crash sites, with the exceptions described below.

Six months later, I returned with angelic beings to the scenes. At the WTC, where considerable work was done to help souls of the dead move on to the light in the weeks following the tragedy, there were no souls present. This is amazing for a place where so many appeared to have died in states of physical shock. But spirit teachers have told me that all who died had that possibility in their life contracts, so they did not die as victims but as teachers for us, for the spiritual growth and expansion of consciousness of people in the United States and around the world.

At the Pentagon, the angelic beings with me found the entities of twelve people, hiding throughout the building in various states of shock, having been blasted from the point of impact. The angels took all of them to the light of Heaven.

At the crash site in Pennsylvania, only one entity remained — that of one of the terrorists, crouched in shock at the base of a tree, not knowing what had happened to him. All others had moved safely to the light. Some might feel that the "bad guys" should suffer, but none of us can know the life purpose of another soul, except for God and the individual soul. And I was not there to judge but to help. In a short time, he was on his way to the light, where he would be able to review details of his entire life and know whether being a "terrorist" (persecutor) was part of his chosen life path or whether his leaders had victimized him.

Shocks to perception and emotions may remain unresolved following death from a natural disaster, even for those that go to the light, such that they remain issues to be carried forward and worked out in another life. A client complained of intermittent pains in her right arm. During regression to the root cause, she became aware of a large weight pressing down her right arm and side. As she brought the scene into clearer detail, she identified the weight as a large boulder that during a past life had fallen from a cliff and crushed her arm and side. Her healer-self was able, through her powers of imagination in the present, to heal the pains of her arm and side and the unresolved emotions of her past-life self.

A woman with a screaming fear of snakes, when regressed to the event of the root cause of her terror, in whatever lifetime, went back about 2,000 years to a time when she was being tortured in a pit of snakes to break her strength of character and Christian faith. She understood the truth of her fear of snakes, and saw that those who caused her death in that lifetime were doing what they believed was right. She was able to forgive them for her death, which resolved her issues in that lifetime and this. Two nights later she had a dream of snakes, which previously would have caused her horror, in which she was able to confront a "huge" snake, learn its true identity, and understand its teaching about her powers of transformation.

Confusion

During depossessions, I encountered spirit entities that were confused about who and what they were. Most were unaware that they had died, their confusion a result of dying under the influence of alcohol, overdose on illegal drugs or prescribed drugs, and anesthetics during surgery (the deaths were not caused by anesthesia, but by the trauma or disease that required the surgery). This does not include suicides. Some deaths resulted from drugs reportedly intended for pain control. One might think a drugged state would be preferable to continual pain, but when drugs are given to the point that clarity of mind is reduced and the person is unaware of what is happening, the death appears to leave unresolved issues to be worked out in a next life — and may leave the soul stuck here, lonely and wandering. Suicides who die of drug overdose have similar experiences.

An entity that reports confusion due to drugs will usually report an inability to see or understand the meaning of the light. This may be an indication of the entity being a fragment of the physical soul. Having a clear mind and attaining a measure of peace, a state of grace before death, appears to be of great importance for a successful transition (Elisabeth Kubler-Ross, *Death: The Final Stage of Growth,* 1975). I would add coming into contact with one's higher self (spirit) and divine self (soul) before death to this list of important final events.

Unfinished Business

Many people with great personal willpower stay on the physical plane because of unfinished business. During depossessions, I have encountered souls of mothers attached to their children. In their anguish over how their children would survive following their deaths, they chose to stay. Also, I have encountered souls of relatively newlywed husbands who felt they needed to stay to provide care and protection for young wives; and grandparents with strong attachments to grandchildren stayed to ensure that their legacy endured. But the staying, no matter how considerate, results in both souls becoming stuck and unable to continue their evolution of consciousness.

A fifty-five-year-old woman reported issues of gloom, over-eating, and overweight. Spirit entities were found attached to her. The most willful of them was that of her mother, who had died when the woman was six years old. The mother, who, according to the client, was a large woman, could not stand to leave her little girl, who was without a father. During depossession it became clear that the entity of the mother was addicted to eating, especially sweets, and could control her daughter's mind and actions sufficiently to maintain her addictions. The woman forgave her mother for the habits she had contributed, and said tearful good-byes as her mother went to the light. She said that she had been able to feel her mother with her and had never been surprised by the many people who had remarked during the past twenty years how much she looked and acted like her mother.

Certain business people are so intensely busy that they die unaware and their "business" entity continues on with the paperwork of their "empire," or they die in the midst of demanding to stay due to all the work they have yet to finish. Loved ones often sense whether they are still around, and have asked me to help remind these souls, usually found in their former offices following death, that it is time to go home.

Sacred Life Contract

The following is an example of a spirit entity staying due to vows with another that were written in their life contracts. Both were members of the same soul family. Because of early deaths of one tor the other in past lives, they vowed to spend this present life together as brothers, which became part of their contracts. One, a fifty-year-old male, came as a client. During depossession of attached spirit entities, I learned that the major entity that was attempting active control in the client's life was his twin brother, who had died in the womb. Not knowing how else to complete the contract, he stayed and attached with his brother's growing body. In our session, when the entity became aware that he was blocking both his and his brother's "evolution," he agreed to go home, so I helped them revise their contracts through the "keeper of contracts" residing in the Upper World, and guided him to the light. Both the entity, through the medium, and the client began crying great tears of grief at the moment of separation. The grieving process of the living brother continued for several months, as if his twin brother had died on the day of the depossession. Several years later, I heard from his wife that his life had "bloomed" following that time and that he was doing well.

Stewards of the Land

This is a special category: in my experience, only Native Americans have chosen to stay as stewards of their native land. During vacations and trips, my medium/partner and I used to travel to historical Native-American campsites. There we would light a candle, and drum and rattle, and call to the spirit entities still on the land to speak with us and tell us their stories. On the California coast, one described how he had been present for many generations, which had been his agreed-upon length of stay, but no one had come to replace him, so he stayed on. When I told him there was no one left of his tribe, he was saddened, but thought he would stay for another generation to see what happened.

In western Nevada, near the Humboldt River marshes, which are the final evaporative parts of the huge Pleistocene Lake

Lahontan, which dates back millions of years, another, who had been chief of his tribe, told me that he had been steward of the lands for "270 seasons." Fully aware that no one of his tribal culture remained in the area, he chose nonetheless to stay and watch over the land and animals. A small group of native spirits of his tribe, but of many different times, had collected around him. In the different places, some of the spirits would choose to go to the light and be with their relations when the offer was made to them. Usually, more would stay.

Guiding Spirits Back Home

To some it may seem presumptuous for a physical being to speak or write of guiding spirits home; home in this case being the Upper World or Lower World, whichever place the spirit needs to go in transition from physical life. But this is one of the major tasks of the shaman. As stated by Mircea Eliade (*Shamanism: Archaic Techniques of Ecstasy*, 1974) in his summary of worldwide tribal shamanism:

> …all through Asia and North America, and elsewhere as well, the shaman performs the function of doctor and healer; he announces the diagnosis, goes in search of the patient's fugitive soul, captures it, and makes it return to animate the body it has left. It is always the shaman who conducts the dead person's soul to the underworld, for he is the psychopomp par excellence (p. 182).

> He commands the techniques of ecstasy [trance, dreams, flight] because his soul can safely abandon his body and roam at vast distances, can penetrate the underworld and rise to the sky.… he knows the roads of the extraterrestrial regions. He can go below

and above because he has already been there.... sanctified by his initiation and furnished with his guardian spirits, the shaman is the only human being able to challenge the danger [of losing his way, or his soul] and venture into a mystical geography (p. 182).

Describing the actual role of psychopomp of Siberian shamans, Eliade reports:

[For the Altaians, Goldi, Yurak]... the shaman escorts the deceased to the beyond at the end of the funeral banquet, while among others (Tungus) he is summoned to fill this role of psychopomp only if the dead man continues to haunt the land of the living beyond the usual period (p. 209).

Among the world's tribes, the timing of funerals varies from the day of death to three, seven, or even longer afterward, for the funeral is the tribes' way of indicating to the soul that it is time to be gone.

In our culture, we no longer understand the purpose of the funeral. We are told it is a time of saying goodbye to the physical body and getting back to our lives. In truth it is a time of spiritual separation: our souls from their soul; and it is a time to grieve our physical loss of their spiritual self. The purpose of the presence of the physical body — from which the spirit has already separated and the upper soul may have completed its separation, as discussed in Chapter Five — is to provide an effigy representing the spirit and soul of the "departed." But this also is a time of joy, a time of celebration that the soul is on its way home. The complete ritual would need to include an opportunity for a shaman as psychopomp to conduct the soul to the light.

Most of my experience as psychopomp has come when loved ones of the deceased, feeling some sense of the presence of a spirit, have called to ask if the soul is still around, and if so, to help it go where it needs to go. This is usually an easy matter. I request that my power animal take me in shamanic journey to the location of the deceased's soul, often found hovering around a loved one or a loved place. I converse with them, pointing out that loved ones will be able to care for themselves, that any "unfinished" business will be taken care of, and that what they need to continue their life's evolution is to let go their attachment to the physical and move on to the spiritual planes, to be with loved ones who have gone before. I ask for the help of an angelic being, then ask the archangel Gabriel for the opening of a portal of light to which we deliver the soul. Speaking the name of a loved one brings the spirit of that person to the portal to greet the newcomer. The archangel Gabriel, who watches over those in transition, will be at or near the portal. Other previously deceased friends and family of the one in transition will come in celebration to welcome the immortal soul back home. Sylvia Browne (*Conversations With The Other Side*, 2002) describes this process in some detail, including the presence of pets and other animal friends who have passed on.

Much less common in this culture is the call to a shaman at the time of death. A few years ago I received a call from a woman whose husband had had a heart attack and was being maintained on life support. She reported that there seemed to be some intermittent brain activity, but her psychic information was that her beloved husband had departed the body. She asked me to see what I could find. I called my spirit helpers and asked them to take me in journey to his soul. I found him sitting in his office and going through papers. I asked what he was doing and he replied that he had gone out to dinner with his wife but had so much work to do that he felt he had to return to the office. I asked if he remembered the details of the dinner and he said he did. I asked if he had experienced any pain during dinner. He said no, but remembered not feeling well, with everything swirling around, and then he came to his office. I asked him to look closely at that moment and remember what had happened, so he did, and remarked in surprise, "I died, didn't I?" I said yes, and he began laughing and said, "Now I'll never get this paperwork done, just like she told me."

I said I would take him where he needed to go. He wanted to go to the hospital, so we flew to the ER. There he stood beside his body and looked at it for a moment, then patted it on the shoulder and turned to his wife, who was sitting in a chair beside the bed. He put his arms around her and said, "I love you." He kissed her at the same time that she stood up, bent over her husband's body, and kissed him, whispering, "Goodbye." We stood, watching as she left the room, and then I delivered him to the archangel Gabriel and the light, where he was met by his father, who had died six months before, and his grandmother. I phoned the wife and told her what I had experienced. She cried and said she knew he was gone, but thought she felt him in the room with her at the last minute. Within a few days the life-support system was withdrawn.

I have learned from the many entities I have encountered while performing depossessions, and from the people they were attached to, that most did not understand the processes of dying or what would happen at death. The majority did not know that at death they would separate from the physical body and be in a spirit body. In America there is little training for death or for the process of dying. In the new spirituality, dying will be a process of heightened awareness and revelation, with loving and understanding separation from loved ones and family, and there will be understanding that our "family" as we grow older may be totally different from the biological family into which we were born. Pain control, where pain is an active part of the dying process, will be learned through self-hypnosis and the shamanic journey to a teacher about pain. Death will be a joyous celebration, a wondrous process and ritual of transition from physical to spiritual life, a "going home."

The New Spirituality

In the new spirituality souls will no longer "have" to remain on Earth to complete unfinished business, or to get even. They will understand that there is nothing they have to do; there is only whom they choose to be. Of course, they will be doing something, for people will always be doing something. "Doing" follows a conscious or unconscious choice of "being." Even when people are unaware of their state of being, it is the root cause of their doing. But if they feel they "have" to do something, or feel "driven" to do something, then their doing is driving them, which is precisely backwards, and is what most of us have been taught: "Go to college, get a degree, get a job, work hard, and *be* happy." It does not work that way. When a state of being that resonates with the heart is chosen, however, such as "I am truth," then the doing will flow from that and be supported by guides, helpers, teachers, and angels of the spirit realm.

The next chapter describes details of possession by spirits, whether entities or entire souls. Most information is concerned with the ability of entities to control our mind and actions, and to interfere with our free will, adding their impulses to those of our dark side. Other issues are examined, such as voluntary possession, which is practiced by shamans, possession of animals by entities, and possession by extraterrestrials.

Chapter Seven

Possession by Spirits

Symptoms of Possession

The following list of the ten most common signs of possession
is from *The Unquiet Dead* by Edith Fiore (1987):

- Low energy level
- Character shifts or mood swings
- Inner voice(s) speaking to you
- Abuse of drugs (including alcohol)
- Impulsive behavior
- Memory problems
- Poor concentration
- Sudden onset of anxiety or depression
- Sudden onset of physical problems with no obvious cause
- Emotional and/or physical reactions to reading The Un-
  quiet Dead [or this book]

Fiore also points out that "addictive" behaviors, behaviors
that people have "given themselves up to" or taken on as habits,
are part of this list.

From my experience, addictions occur in personal areas such as:

- INTAKE: food, sweets, alcohol, drugs (prescribed and illegal), tobacco, coffee.
- OUTPUT: work, sex, sloth, criminal actions.
- PASTIMES: sports, games, gambling, reading, TV.
- HYPOCHONDRIA: habitual or constant feelings and symptoms of illnesses that lack organic cause, possibly leading to disability (physical and legal sense); fatigue and exhaustion with varying degrees of pain, (similar to fibromyalgia); feeling very old and painful while young; feeling sure that one is dying when no other symptoms exist.

I would add that these addictions, when caused or emphasized by entities, are usually in sufficient excess that a health issue or threat to life may result.

Involuntary Possession

Involuntary spirit possession is a situation in which a spirit entity attaches in a parasitic relationship with a human being. According to the biblical accounts of possession in Chapter Three, in ancient Judea this involuntary relationship with spirits was the root cause of convulsions, "fits," craziness, and the "blunting" of abilities to see, hear, and speak. Living and health conditions were different then. The lower class of people with whom Jesus associated lived in crowded, unhealthy conditions, drawing upon communal water sources with a high probability of contamination from nearby sewage, and lacking access to medical care, available only to the rich. Therefore, outward signs of possession were probably more severe than in our present-day culture. Public displays of possession may have been commonplace, with the exhibition of more evident symptoms than now, such that most people knew when someone was possessed by a spirit or demon, and may have felt the situation to be beyond help.

Today, in this country, instances of people acting out publicly in some bizarre fashion are rarer, probably due to medication. Quite common are those who appear to be "street people" walking along, pushing a shopping cart, and arguing with some unseen, unknown "other." The same form of dialog can be seen among enraged drivers during commute hours. I have seen similar situations in the day rooms of convalescent and psychiatric hospitals when I led groups in those places; also, in the early-morning solitary drinker on the corner bar stool. But most possessed by spirit entities cause no overt social problems.

In *The Unquiet Dead* (1987), Edith Fiore estimated 75 percent of our population have possessing spirit entities. I concur that the number is at least that high. Most of these spirit entities are gentle and mild mannered, but still drain life-force energy from their hosts and add their emotional confusion and agendas to the minds of their hosts. A small percentage are very strong willed, apparently capable of controlling thought and action, some without conscience, and are dangerous to the host person and society. Of the more than 500 clients I saw for shamanic healing from early 1997 through 2000, approximately 85 percent came bringing attached spirit entities, and received depossession as part of their healing. During 2001, apparently due to clients' word-of-mouth stories of their relief from depossessions and exorcisms, the number increased to nearly 100 percent and has remained at that level.

The following is a typical example of possession. A client related, "I remember this strange experience of riding with my husband to a new town. As we went through a particular intersection I began screaming and I could feel agony in my body as if I were in a wreck. That was ten years ago. Now, finally, I understand what happened, and why after that I always felt some unknown anxiety when driving through an intersection."

During the depossession, in dialog with me through the client's voice, the spirit entity whose physical body had died in an accident at that intersection reported that it had stayed around the intersection "for a long time," continually feeling the shock and terror of the wreck. Then, along came this woman who, it sensed, had great sympathy for people's suffering, and instantly the spirit entity attached to her.

Spirit entities are the souls, or fragments of souls, of humans whose physical bodies have died but which, through choice or terror or confusion, stayed on Earth (Chapters Five and Six). Spirit entities attach to a person's body and mind to feel alive again. The simplest way is to see life through someone's physical eyes. Once physical vision is restored, the fact of physical death can be denied. Over time and through will a spirit entity can energetically merge with a person's mental and emotional systems to a degree that they can monitor the thoughts, know the memories, and feel the emotions of their host. They become another "voice" in the person's head. The voice, depending on the intent, will, and unmet needs of the spirit entity — its addictions and obsessions — may encourage the host to engage in some action: "Let's have another cookie, they're small." Or, "Let's have another drink, it's early." For the entity determined to play out drama as a victim, "Pick up on that guy, he looks rough and tough." And when something bright catches the eye of a former thief, now entity, "Look — a diamond, and no one's watching." The action may grow into habit or addiction without any awareness that the impulse being carried out is due to the will of another being.

Spirit entities first attach to the outer layers of the aura, a person's invisible and subtle energetic body. Over time, through distortions and tears in the aura's structure, they work their way inward in a manner similar to the way that negative thought forms and disease attack a person (Brennan, *Hands Of Light,* 1995), until they are merged with the host's mind. For people who are healed, healthy, and spiritually whole, entities may be able to penetrate no deeper than the outer layer of the aura.

Spirit entities are commonly seen, with clairvoyant sight, or during shamanic journey, attached at the back of the neck, blocking the rear fifth chakra, which is the center of personal willpower and one's ability to speak his or her truth. All holes, tears, or distortions to the structure of the aura, where spirit entities are able to gain entry, occur on the outer surface of the astral or spiritual plane, or to the chakras that have been damaged by life's traumas. An example of fifth-chakra damage would be a young girl or boy who was slapped or yelled at for telling her mother who was jerking her arm in the store, "You're hurting me," or for telling his father when he stumbled home on a Friday night, "You're drunk."

During possession, a spirit entity can provide distorted beliefs to convince the possessed person that he or she is someone else — and that someone else is who the spirit entity was in life. A moderate and usual level of distortion that a spirit entity might try is, "I am trying to help you, and you should listen to me, for I am your friend. You should spend some money now." The voice may be seductively soft and gentle, but different from divine spirit because it will often include demands — "shoulds" and "oughts" — and may include aspects of addiction and obsession. However, the voice may be harsh and abrupt: "You should have another drink." At a more mental level of consciousness, the possessed person may be battered by more than one entity, driving him to distraction with conflicting internal dialog: "Let's go party with the gang." " No, let's go hide out for the week."

Because a spirit entity is usually trapped in an endless mental loop of the actions and emotions of the scene of its death, the possessed person hears these, in some sense, played over and over. The host may learn to shut his mind to the voice(s) by playing background music sufficiently loud that he no longer hears the details, but the energy still is there. When he or she finally lies down to sleep at night, the voice of demand, woe, misery, anger, fear, etc., is there clamoring to be heard. This can increase anxiety levels, stress levels, pulse, and blood pressure, such that the person does not rest or dream healing dreams, and the immune system suffers, inviting illness.

Spirit entities are attracted to people who are like them, or seem opposite to them. In a sense, a codependent relationship forms, similar to many human relationships, where one provides what the other lacks. The human provides physical eyes in trade for the spirit's encouragement to buy attractive things that it sees, and the human provides life-force energy in trade for the company of spirit's voice and not feeling lonely. The human provides social interactions that the spirit entity can feel part of, and provides the ability to go places. The spirit entity provides the emotional enthusiasm or drive to do things, perhaps even those that are risky and exciting. But all of this interaction with a spirit entity may bring new emotions to the relationship that the human attempts to block or deny. This can bring out emotional mood swings, previously unseen in the person that can be quite disconcerting in human relationships. In fact, a good clue to the presence of a possessing spirit entity is when a close friend says, "That wasn't you talking," or "That's not how you usually act."

For example, a client related that she lived a peaceful, quiet life, but one day, while talking with a woman who had been her friend for many years, the friend exploded in anger at her "over nothing." She felt herself blameless. In dialog with the possessing spirit, I discovered that my client was hosting a spirit entity that manipulated others into outbursts of anger so it could feed on the feeling of being a victim, its favorite position in what has been called the "drama triangle" of victim-persecutor-rescuer.

During dialog with the spirit entity, preparatory to depossession, I found that both women had attended a meeting where anger ran high among many present. The client exhibited fear, which attracted the spirit entity that had been attached to another. After the client reported the relief of depossession to her friend, she too came as a client. During dialog with the spirit entity attached to her, I found that she too had attracted a spirit entity at the same gathering. Her spirit entity also was female with a zest for verbal violence. She not only manipulated people into angry exchanges, but also fed off the explosive emotional peaks of energy of her human host to feel stronger and more alive. This spirit entity was much more verbally forceful about wanting to stay on Earth, "to stay with her." She did not want me "messing with her life." After some negotiation where the advantages of being with loved ones and being healed were pointed out, she took the hand of her mother reaching down to her and went to the portal of light.

A spirit entity, soul or soul fragment, from a person who died after lengthy debilitating and painful disease, such as cancer or AIDS, may deluge the host with endless repetition of its symptoms. These feelings may convince the host that he or she has the same symptoms, or even disease, much the same way that medical students may feel they exhibit symptoms of diseases they are studying.

Spirit entities may attach to a person in the vain attempt to resolve past-life issues with that person. Baldwin (*Spirit Releasement Therapy,* 1995) cites the case of a client with a physical symptom; when asked to return to the first occasion when the symptom occurred, the client regressed to a past life. The memory of both the past- and the present-life symptoms was of the spirit entity attached to the client. Also, the spirit entity had an unresolved issue with the client during that past life. It had waited for the person to incarnate again to attempt to continue the relationship. When the possessing spirit was healed of the unresolved issues and could understand that there was no value staying around in this life, it released from the person and went to the light.

In my work, I have found it useful to assign names to certain types of spirit entities, to remind myself of the kinds of stress the spirit would likely subject the client to; and to highlight the types of spirits that create the greatest personal and social problems for people.

"Demonic" Spirit Entities

"Demonic" spirit entities are spirits, not demons, although I believe all are under control of a shape-shifting giant demon. They are rare, but when exposed, which they do not like, they want to be called "devil." Some have told me that a priest gave them that name during an exorcism; several have boasted that the name was deserved due to murders they committed while in human form. Commonly, each tried to arouse my fears by threatening me, in voices of rage and hate, with bodily injury. Their intent, I believe, is domination of the human they possess, so they can direct the host into the kinds of relationships with which the spirits are obsessed: power, sex, abuse, humiliation, tyranny, etc.

What differentiates these demonic-type entities from demons, discussed later, is that they can be spoken with; they answer questions in apparent truth, in contrast to demons that only lie (until encapsulated in a "super bubble filled with light"). They are usually fragments of some person's lower physical soul, the shadow self, retaining impulses and urges of the person's dark side. The ones I spoke with had all been around for a long time, from 300 to more than 1,000 years. Many had been put to death for crimes and stayed on Earth "to get even" with those they blamed for their deaths. Each was afraid that an invitation to go to the light was a trap to take it to hell. Therefore, it was imperative to assure them that there is no hell, that it was a religious invention to keep people in fear.

No exorcist should encounter a demonic-type or potentially dangerous spirit without advance warning or experience, which is why I teach students to divine, to make a determination of the types of spirits (and demons) that are attached to a person before encountering them. I recommend, when a demonic-type spirit is present, whether in face-to-face or distance healing, that the angelic beings be called to bring a light-filled bubble to enclose the spirit (and a super bubble filled with light for the demon) and to tighten it so the spirit cannot move or harm anyone. It will go to the light when love and truth pull the force out of its rampaging arguments. Only rarely do I enter into dialog with demonic-type spirit entities (or demons).

"Sorcerer" Spirit Entities

Spirit entities that I have termed "sorcerers" also are rare. All have been male, in my experience, which is not to say that all sorcerers are male. Their deaths occurred during the past 1,000 years, mostly during the Inquisition, when they were tried as sorcerers, found guilty, and killed. In initial dialog with sorcerer-type spirit entities, however, they usually tried to convince me of their helping practices as healer, alchemist, metaphysician, astrologer, herbalist, or some helping art. That may have been the truth for some of those wrongly accused, not uncommon during times of the Inquisition. Only with some interrogation did any negative practices emerge, usually some form of the black arts, controlling another person's body or soul through curses or through control of other spirit entities that could control another's body and soul. They seemed to be attracted to possession of people who play the role of "pawn" during life, so they can move them around on the "gameboard" while remaining invisible in the background. I believe that most are in the secret control of a giant demon.

All were stuck on Earth for two reasons: one, "to get even" by making people suffer for their death (the precise details of how were unclear, but they generally made the humans they possessed miserable by tormenting them); and two, for "unfinished business," that of collecting people's souls, and fragments of souls, in order to have power over those people. They hated the thought of going to the light as they felt that "life" as invisible spirits on Earth was better than before and didn't want to give it up. On several occasions in dialog during shamanic journey with a sorcerer-type, an angelic being came up to the spirit entity, wrapped its wings tightly around it, and whispered, "Your time of game playing on Earth is finished. Now is the time for coming Home to be healed. Talk to this man and tell him your story so you can be healed. You are loved." For once I, a human, had intervened with the spirit entity, the angelic realm could become directly involved in moving the entity in the direction of its highest good.

Before sorcerer-type spirit entities go to the light, it is important that they release all souls and soul fragments to the rightful beings. Once the sorcerer type agrees to let go of its accumulation, I call the guardian angels of all whose souls or fragments it is holding, so each may be returned to the rightful entity. The transfer procedure is instantaneous regardless of when in time the soul or fragment is from.

"Bully" Entities

A bully type, as the word implies, is a persecutor. Usually, a bully pushes people around in anger to cover its underlying fears and lack of self-esteem. Bully-type spirit entities do the same. I have seen both male and female. One of their favorite sports is to attach with someone of the opposite sex and drive away all of his or her suitors, so they can keep the person as "their own." Or, they encourage the person to get involved in many sexual affairs that they could not experience during their own lives. Also, as Edith Fiore (*The Unquiet Dead*, 1987) indicates, possession by an opposite-sex entity can cause confusion about sexual identity in the possessed person.

Bully-type spirits especially push around people who play the role of "victim" on this game-board of life. Such people may feel "pushed" into making decisions that lead to pain, into getting involved in situations they did not intend, or into giving up personal power to another when they knew they shouldn't. Spirits of this nature are readily open to truth, caring, and love, and will usually go to the light with little effort.

The demonic type, the sorcerer type, and the bully type are no more real than the labels given to any other classification. I use those forms so I can generalize, both when talking to clients about the nature of possessing spirit entities and when writing. These are the strong-willed types, who have strong emotions and wills to get their way with the people they attach with. Precisely how much they get their way is a matter of some conjecture, but largely unknown.

In my experience, the weaker-willed spirit entities — the victim type, the pawn type, and the passive-aggressive type (from "weakest" to "strongest") — seem to be the cause of little discomfort to their human hosts. Still, they use the host's energy, pour out their emotional tales of woe, and are entangled with the host's mind such that some of their habits and beliefs "rub off," so the impact may be greater than we want to acknowledge. Many of these stay stuck on Earth due to dying in confusion, terror, and shock, as described in Chapter Six.

A spirit entity's control over a person's mind and/or actions has a very wide range. It is countered by the strength of the person's willpower, so it may be imperceptible to very strong, partial to total, and intermittent to frequent. In my experience spirit entities have been known to control the conscious ego mind, block the free will, and add to urges and impulses of the dark side of the subconscious mind. Possession may be the root cause of, or exacerbate, addictions and actions such as alcohol and drug abuse, violence and physical abuse, sexual abuse (of all kinds, including that between married couples), overeating, suicide, criminal activities, and mental illness. The strength of control of a possessing spirit entity over a living person appears to be dependent on the spirit's force of will relative to the strength of will and level of awareness of the host, and on its emotional reason for being stuck on Earth.

Control of the Mind and Body

As incredible as it seems, the personality of the invisible spirit entity remains little changed from when it had its own physical body before death. Certainly, after attaining a level of enlightenment from inner work, during and between lives, which may require many lifetimes, "spiritual awakening" may occur. But while stuck on Earth, as an entity, whether soul fragment or entire soul, there is no change in personality from before death. The one who during life played the role of a meek victim remains so after death, and the authoritarian male or female also remains so. The violence prone, the alcohol abuser, the overeater, the sexually addicted, the criminal, the sufferer of tyrannies of the dark side, all retain their proclivities while stuck on Earth in spirit form. Some are very demanding about having their needs met, and at any time of day or night, as a possessing spirit no longer is concerned with the physical concept of time.

Criminal activities are known to be encouraged or directed by "voices in the head." In discussion groups that I have led in jail or prison, these are given as excuses for crimes. Voices of possessing spirit entities range from a soft-voiced encouragement to steal ("Oh, go ahead, they'll never miss it"), to the demanding voice of "Sam the Terrible," which David Berkowitz (the "Son of Sam") alleged directed him to commit mass murder. The voices may seductively or demandingly override any personal conscience existing in the ego of the possessed person.

Over the years, as in the movie *The Shining*, Jack Nicholson has convincingly portrayed possession by strong-willed spirit entities. The voice of the host is used by any entity with sufficient will to take over the vocal cords. A different voice may break out of the host as a separate personality indulging in (obsessing with) long, rambling, crazy monologues. To what degree human activities can be totally controlled by possessing spirit entities is unknown.

One summer evening, a few years before I knew much about this "business," I was driving my car relatively fast on a mountainous highway in northern California over which I had driven many times. I was relaxed, feeling very alive, and looking forward to a few days of relaxation. As I came down a long sweeping curve to the left, with a sharp drop on my right into a valley 300 feet below, I felt hands take each of my forearms and abruptly twist the steering wheel to the right in an adrenaline-rushing movement. I snapped my hands back to the left, and said no out loud just as the right front tire dropped over the pavement lip to the dirt shoulder. The car corrected without fishtailing and we (the car, and ?, and I) proceeded down the road — I, at least, shaken by the experience. I have several times since driven that section of highway without incident, but not without a heightened sense of awareness of the possibilities in this world.

Spirits with whom I have spoken in shamanic journey, or through the client as medium, or through an independent medium, are usually reluctant or refuse to say to what extent they control their hosts' mind or actions. One spirit entity, however, was directed on a mission by a black sorcerer in a southern city where curses and other dark methods are still practiced. The mission, as the story was grudgingly told to me, was to kill a young man, my client, who knew the sorcerer in control of the entity.

Spirit entities readily admit that they urge their host to stop off at a bar and have a drink, or to have another piece of cake late at night. Usually, they will admit that anger turns them on, and may admit to encouraging the host into arguments. Even the mildest spirit entities feed off the energy of human emotional outbursts to feel more alive, bigger, and more powerful. This is decidedly a drain on the host.

One of the many possible causes of suicide appears to be possession. Based on the experiences of surviving clients, when the mind of the possessed person was so incessantly tormented or terrorized by the chaos of a possessing spirit, finding no other relief, they attempted to kill themselves. But suicide is a no-win situation. Those who die that way can become stuck on Earth as entities, or they reincarnate almost immediately, without any period of healing to have a second opportunity at the same life situation.

Interfering with Free Will

A person has free will when all of his or her mind is available to make the choice, that is, conscious mind, subconscious mind, and superconscious mind are available to evaluate information and make choices. Spirit entities interfere with the exercise of free will by placing themselves as energetic blocks between the ego self and divine self (the upper soul), between the awareness of the conscious mind and the superconscious mind. The energetic block can do a variety of things (most of them unknown due to little study), such as cause static interference, like white noise, disrupting internal thought so that a single "track" cannot be followed for more than a moment before another thought interferes; insert foreign emotions and "voices" to provide contrary and self-serving advice to a person; and sometimes masquerade as the person's conscience, spirit teacher, or higher self. As Fiore points out, confusion and loss of memory are the usual symptoms.

Most people who have learned to meditate, or tried to learn, know how difficult it is to turn off thinking of the conscious mind. I seldom begin meditation without finding myself rambling off on some unintentional tangent of thought. To shut out that thinking, people customarily and habitually play music or turn on television, even when in another room, to provide "white noise" to block out the "chatter" of other voices.

The voice of divine spirit, whether from our guides, angels, spirit teachers, higher self, or God, is very soft and gentle, so much so that even a TV with the sound muted will block the voice, for spirit has no intention, or permission, to interrupt the operation of a person's free will: watching TV, listening to music, arguing with neighbors, yelling at the kids. Spirit provides advice when asked or prayed for, before a choice is made, but the person must be quiet and very focused to hear the voice. Experience and dedication, as well as intent and focus, are required to walk along in nature and hear the voice of spirit. People who grow up in tune with the rhythms and signs of nature are open to receiving the messages from soul and spirit, but in the urban environment it's nearly impossible to hear, let alone learn to listen, to one's soul or spirit. Quiet is required, but most people have no idea that this means not answering phones because they are turned off; not listening to music because the stereo is off; that one's family understand the meaning of a closed door; that one settles into a posture of silence where learning can begin, if only for one evening a week.

Spirit will not argue against a choice once made. There is no last-second intercession to stop a person from pulling the trigger of a pistol pressed against his temple with the intention of ending life — even when he realizes in the last microsecond, as the finger applies the last ounce of pressure, that he judged himself wrongly and is not guilty. Spirit will not say, "Stop!" To do so would interfere with the progress of personal soul and human free will. This is why some people falsely believe that prayers are not answered. Spirit honors all our intentions in the moment given, but spirit does not do the things that are not to be done. In rare cases, though, the hand twitches (is twitched?) or the bullet travels around the skull rather than through it, and the person is given another opportunity to continue his life's path. These "miracles" occur because death, at that point and in that way, was not in the person's life contract. Therefore, protection was provided by his or her guardian angel.

After a person makes a choice from free will — "I'm going to live a spiritual life," "I'm going to give up drinking and take care of my family responsibilities," "I'm going to become [educated, rich, available] to help people": or, "I'm going to get drunk and stay drunk," "I'm going to practice the dark arts," then spirit is again freely available to help the person with advice, with co-creation of daily reality, with orchestration of synchronous events, and providing signs and signals from nature to show the person they are following their path. For spirit there is no judgment of the choice, no good or bad, no right or wrong.

I have worked with a number of women clients who report the desire but the inability to have a relationship of any duration with a man. In each case a male spirit entity with a jealous, possessive nature, with a coyote-like ability to sabotage a budding romance, was the root cause. After depossession or exorcism, those of these women whose situations I was kept informed of were usually able to form a relationship with a man. The amount of time it took to find a relationship that felt "right" ranged from the same month as the healing work to several years.

A somewhat different example of a lack of free will is the following. In 1996, a man's concerned friends referred him to me because "he looked like he was going to hurt someone." After a glance at his menacing appearance, I suggested we talk on the front lawn. Within moments he was crouched like an attack dog, screaming at me about all the people he had killed over many years, about the ways he was going to kill me to keep me from the work I was doing. Amidst his screams I began speaking to him, which seemed to infuriate him even more, but I continued. I don't remember the words I spoke, but the sense was "When you stop screaming, I'll help you." Finally, after a time, he wound down and said, abruptly, that he had an appointment in town and had to leave. He agreed to return the following day, but never came back — again a sign of a lack of free will. Of course, there are other possibilities: perhaps the man was healed, by himself and spirit, and went his way laughing and singing; perhaps the possessing being was a demon, and he went and attacked someone more to his choosing.

But if a person is pressured by his or her peer group to start smoking, or rob a convenience store, or join AA, or go to church, then isn't his free will being interfered with? No, for spirit considers these people to be operating from free will despite being strong-armed by peers. The person might later complain of having had no choice. However, through the ages, other people faced with the same choices have chosen to die or suffer public disgrace or loss of friends in order to speak their truth and maintain their freedom of choice and way of life. Some people seem to be "locked in" to a path where choices are not free. In my experience, the choices and life decisions that result in the appearance of being locked in to a narrow path were made years previous, usually between the ages of two and eight, as the result of an emotional wounding.

An example is a forty-two-year-old woman client who came to quit drinking and stop beating her child. Her life path was comparable to that of many people whose childhood had been similar to hers, but on the other hand, many with similar childhood lead very different lives. She was the oldest child, her father's pride. By age five, for survival as much as love, she decided, based on a beating she received from her father, to be like him (who smoked, drank, and exploded unpredictably into rage). At age eight she smoked a cigarette, for which she was severely beaten by her enraged father ("because you're too young to smoke"), and by twelve she was secretly getting drunk on beer given by her uncle at parties. By seventeen she was smoking and drinking, had a tough reputation, and was avoided for her explosive temper. At each successive stage she made the choice to stay on the path of being like her father, and was supported in her choices by several entities that were similar to him. Most had attached with her during the confusing time of puberty, when her self-image came in conflict with her changing biology. But the reasons for her life choices became clearer to the woman when she could understand that her childhood decision, later supported by the entities, prevented her making other choices.

Adding to Dark-side Impulses

Within the subconscious mind, the part of the self that we cannot access in ordinary consciousness, lives the dark side of the self. Carl Jung (*Memories, Dreams, Reflections*; 1961, p. 235) termed the "dark side of the being" as being an individual's "sinister shadow." Jung's inspiration and courage to work with his own shadow and those of his clients showed that it "contains the hidden, repressed, and unfavorable or nefarious aspects of the personality." Jung characterized one of man's life battles as between the ego and the shadow, analogous to the archetypal struggles between the hero and the dragon. His experience showed that if the shadow is repressed, through fear, mistrust, religion, parental teaching, then part of a person's supply of psychic energy is bound in storage and unavailable or lost for life. In that case the person cannot achieve his greatest potential. Jung's premise underlies my present work with clients.

Our personal dark side consists of all the actions and behaviors and emotions that were prohibited, usually by our parents and grandparents, as they came into expression. At the penetrating sound of "No," or "Don't," they become stuffed, without ever having known form or experience, without having registered on our consciousness as anything but bad, into what Robert Bly, in *The Little Book on the Shadow* (1988), called "the bag you drag around behind you." There they become impulses and urges that ferment until perceived provocations threaten our core beliefs, our "sacred cows," or when pressures are sufficiently great to trigger an emotional explosion. The longer and tighter the dark side has been stuffed, the greater the fermenting process and the chance for explosion. Then tragic events like beatings, rape, torture, and murder can occur.

Spirit entities, and demons (to be discussed in later chapters), find a ready doorway to us as long as we remain fearful of our dark side and in judgment of the dark sides of others. What we fear is attracted to us. If our family taught us that anger is bad, not allowed (except by father or mother "gods" of our home), then we deny our anger, fear anger, and perennially attract to us situations and relationships that bring anger into our lives. Angry and enraged spirit entities, those I term "demonic," will see fear or anger within as an open invitation to take up residence. To feel more alive and more powerful, they will provoke a person into angry situations or outbursts. Children who are prohibited from expressing sadness, excitement, leadership ("bossiness"), concern, nurturing, closeness (touching, hugging), joy (spontaneous wild yells and screams), and body noises and functions, are vulnerable to fears of exposing this part of themselves due to guilt or shame. These parts of self join the hidden content of their dark side.

The dark side of self is easy to know, even when one is in denial of one's "terrible and horrible" impulses. Sometimes these behaviors are shown in dreams, most likely as metaphors for personal learning. Read the front page of a newspaper or watch TV news. Whatever causes you to suck in your breath, mutter "that's horrible," become secretly titillated or aroused, or angry, is a part of your repressed dark side. Whenever you look at another person, watch TV, or read the newspaper and think of a person's actions as "horrible," "dirty," or "evil," you are projecting your dark side onto those people. Since September 11, 2001, there has been no shortage of examples of the human dark side and human judgment of the dark side. The shadow is a reflection of your own dark side on someone else. Of course, our shadow also has its light elements, as Jung has pointed out. You may project "blithe spirit" on a woman you see skipping along the sidewalk or singing with joy, "courage" on a man who speaks out against injustice or hugs another man, or "smiling angel" on a friendly child. All are projections of the light side of yourself, repressed within as a part of yourself, but seen and admired mostly in the mirrors of strangers.

There is a darker side to the dark side. I believe that all who are in this realm are controlled by entities (and driven by demons). These are the people who actively study, experiment with, and develop their dark sides in their pursuit of power over, greed, or lust. They may operate alone, or be "cult" leaders. Whichever, their darkest behaviors will be in secret, and this secret may be the core around which a cult or "secret" organization is formed. The core behaviors usually are ones that are "beyond the pale," meaning criminal. The behaviors may start out with a child experimenting with the "disassembly" of a pet to "see how it runs," but probably attempting to understand death. In most children, I believe that a single instance of discovering the capability of their dark side will be the end of experimentation. But in some, where possessing demonic-type spirits, or demons and / or the dark forces (see Chapter Thirteen), have been waiting for the person to become old enough in this new incarnation to be active participants again, experimentation may escalate to torturing or killing tame animals, hurting or cutting on their own body, or hurting and cutting on someone else's. In the adult version, this may or may not lead to mass torture and killing, such as the Holocaust, to cult killings and torture, to serial murder, serial rape, and incest. These same behaviors have been in this world since long before Sodom and Gomorrah.

Even David, King of Judea — with good cause, due to his lust for another man's wife — sang to God to be protected from his dark side, which he knew was present: "Don't let me lust for evil things; don't let me participate in acts of wickedness. Don't let me share in the delicacies of those who do evil." (Ps. 141:4).

Ronna Herman, as a channel for the archangel Michael (*The Golden Promise*, 2001), a messenger from God to us on Earth in this "now" age, reports him as saying:

The shadow side of life on Earth is roiling and bubbling to the surface as each of you, individually and collectively, are given the opportunity to look in the mirror of life and face the fears and imperfections you have created – an opportunity to heal core pattern distortions with love and understanding.... Know that when you are judging others, you are also judging yourselves. You must each turn within and face your shadow-side and as you do so without fear or judgment, with love and compassion, miracles begin to happen. As a bold Light Warrior, you must face your worst enemy, your own shadow self (p. 352).

The truth of the dark side for most is that there is nothing bad there, nothing evil, except possibly the fear of it. The misperception and judgment of it usually originates in childhood. Shining the light of consciousness on it, eliminating secrets and denial, eliminates the shadow. Regression to the event, whether in this or a previous life, usually allows the perception of the event through adult eyes to clarify misperceptions of the child, thus healing what was kept secret. Another way of acknowledging is to tell someone who will not judge your secret, about the worst things you have done to another person. This is well and simply stated in the fifth step of AA: "Admitted to God, to ourselves, and to another human being the exact nature of our wrongs."

The purpose of bringing the dark side into enlightened consciousness is that within the dark side may be locked up your creative expression, your personal power, and your passion for life. They become released and available by exploring them through the arts and communicating them — by writing poetry, composing and singing or playing music, painting, journal writing, dancing, writing fiction or nonfiction — rather than by avoiding and denying.

Animals and Extraterrestrials

According to reports from those purporting to know, Extraterrestrials (ETs) are around us on Earth as invisible discarnate beings. They will come to people who, in the adventurous nature of this new age, call for them. But not all appear to have the highest or best interests of humans at "heart." I have been told, by the few I have communicated with, that many are here observing human emotions because they are not everywhere present, and they are not above putting people in negative emotional situations to observe the reactions. They do not honor Earth laws of free-will choice that are universally honored by benevolent spirits and higher spiritual beings. Also, they may not honor directives to return to their homes or leaders. I have found that they may leave momentarily and then return to continue their missions. The ETs I have spoken with recently have turned out to be shape-shifting giant demons, disguised to confuse humans.

Further information about ETs is available from the various organizations now involved with, and in the study of, extraterrestrials, such as the Center for Study of Extraterrestrial Intelligence (CSETI) founded by Dr. Steven Greer (www.cseti.org). Recent channeled information indicates that the time may be near when benevolent ETs will be appearing in this country (Rother, *Welcome Home*, 2002).

In the past I found what appeared to be ETs attached with animals, similar to the way possessing spirits attach. I received a call from a person whose dog had begun barking continuously and crazily for no apparent reason. In a journey to the animal, a being reporting to be an ET was found attached to the dog's head. This being explained that it was on a mission to observe

135

the family, and it could not leave because it did not have permission from its group leader. Finally, it agreed to leave to tell its commander that the laws of free will must be obeyed on Earth. It did not return immediately, but I suspect that another dog soon began barking wildly for no reason.

I received an intriguing call from the owner of six valuable horses, all in various stages of EPM (equine poliomyelitis) with varying atrophy of the muscles of their backs and hind legs. In shamanic journeys to the spirits of the horses, I found that intrusions (negative thought forms) were the root cause. The source of the cause was the spirit of a Native-American elder who had been killed along with all of his tribal group by gold miners in the Sierras who were out for a little Sunday sport during the 1850s. He and "his woman" stayed at the site, but all others had "disappeared." Then, 140 years later, this family came along and started building barns and corral fences all over their camps and sacred sites. Each time the old couple would settle in one place, they would be disturbed and have to move. Finally, the old man told me that he got angry and yelled to the people, "If you don't get off my back, I'm going to get on yours," which he did. Over a period of about five months, each of the horses, the family, and family dog developed hip and back conditions.

All the negative energies around had in turn formed a negative vortex directed upward into the solar system. It was used by extraterrestrials in the vicinity as a dumping ground for some unwanted energy forms. When I first made contact with them in shamanic journey, I found them to be in the form of large, slow-moving blobs, able to slowly communicate and follow directions. But they would blunder around the barn and short out, or turn on or off, the electrical systems, further upsetting the ponies. I ordered them back up the vortex to their home, then closed and rolled up the vortex. At their request, I guided the Native-American spirit couple to the light where they could be with their friends and family again. The horses were cleared of negative influences and got better, with the assistance of an herbal healer working to strengthen their immune systems.

Voluntary Possession

Voluntary possession by spirit entities is well known in shamanic tribal cultures, as extensively researched and reported by Mircea Eliade in *Shamanism: Archaic Techniques of Ecstasy* (1974). This appears to be a cultural form among certain shamanic tribes, encouraged for purposes of passing on shamanic power and knowledge from one generation to the next. Many shamanic practitioners trained in advanced healing methods of core shamanism by the Foundation for Shamanic Studies use a form of voluntary possession during certain types of healing. The practitioner calls his or her spirit teacher or spirit helper (possibly both) to come from their location in the Upper or Lower Worlds to the Middle World and merge their spirit with the practitioner's for the healing benefit of the client. When merger is complete, the increase in power (energy available for healing) in the healer is physically apparent to the healer, the client, and to onlookers. When the healing procedure is completed, the practitioner gratefully requests the healing spirit(s) to separate and return to their worlds.

Edgar Cayce, called "The Sleeping Prophet" and the father of holistic medicine, was a great trance channel in this country during the first half of the twentieth century (Henry Reed, *Edgar Cayce: On Channeling Your Higher Self*, 1989). Hypnosis was used as the method to induce his trances, from which state of consciousness he channeled many thousands of individual health remedies and life readings that proved highly accurate and beneficial. Cayce attributed his information to a variety of sources including his higher self and benevolent beings.

Channels are people who voluntarily agree to allow benevolent spirits, angelic beings, ascended masters, councils of wise elders, extraterrestrials, and also their higher selves to use their voices for teachings of self or for the world at large. Probably the best channels are those who have channeling written as a desired life experience in their life contracts. On the other hand, probably everyone can channel.

For some, this practice has been going on for many lifetimes. Some trace their spiritual lineage to the oracles at Delphi who for centuries before the life of Jesus provided wise council for the people of the Grecian and surrounding empires. Examples of channels presently teaching in this country are Barbara Marciniak who channels ETs from the Pleiades (*Earth*), Lee Carroll who channels a being affiliated with the archangel Michael called Kryon (*Kryon, Books 1-9*), Ronna Herman who channels the archangel Michael (*The Golden Promise*), and Steve Rother who channels a council of wise elders called The Group (*Re-Member,* and *Welcome Home*). There are many others.

The agreement between human channel and spirit channel usually has limits and boundaries that are understood to be in the interests of both sides and in the best interests of humanity. However, there have been allegations of fraud surrounding channeling, probably since the time of the Hebrew prophets that channeled God. Unfortunately, there continue to be people without any qualifications who ask for a spirit or extraterrestrial to come speak to or through them. They may well obtain the services of a lost and lonely spirit entity that is not benevolent, or is malevolent, and that lies to the person and creates a permanent attachment. Or they may be answered by an extraterrestrial that is on a mission for purposes other than the person's best interests.

Voluntary possession also is the process used by mediums who speak for spirits of the dead, both those that have gone to the light and those who have remained on Earth. Much of the time their work is performed in séances, in a circle around a table where all place their hands flat on the tabletop. But the work may also be done one on one in individual readings. In a sense mediums provide proof that life goes on following the death of the physical body, and that should provide relief to those who fear that death is the absolute end. Fundamentalist teachings and preachers have maintained that communicating with spirits is the work of the devil. Thus many people remain fearful and skeptical of mediums. True mediums of the New Age have moved away from the pseudo-Gypsy image, and have dropped the elements of high drama as a flavoring to their readings. They provide the public a helpful service by directly reporting the comments and conditions of loved ones who have made the transition from physical life.

In the next chapter, methods of depossession of spirit entities (and demons) are discussed. For those who are interested in entering this type of healing work, suggestions are made for additional areas of study that would benefit practitioners.

Chapter Eight

Depossession of Spirits and Demons

Depossession is the removal of parasitic possessing spirits and demons through:

1. Verbal dialog with the possessing being through a medium, or the client as medium, with or without the use of hypnosis, negotiating with it to leave;

2. Ordering or requesting the possessing being to leave through reading a prepared script;

3. Praying that the possessed person be "delivered" of the possessing being; and

4. Shamanic journey with face-to-face meeting and dialog with the possessing being, to deliver it, or arrange for it to go where it needs.

Depossession can be performed face to face or at a distance. Similar practices by other authors and practitioners are called "clearing," "spirit release," and "deliverance." Some practices are religious rituals, as in the case of the "exorcisms" of the Catholic Church and the "deliverance ministry" of both Protestant and Catholic churches.

Many forms of depossession (and exorcism) are used in the world, particularly in shamanic tribal cultures and Asian cultures as described in *Possession* (Oesterreich, 1966), and *Shamanism* (Eliade, 1974). In my constantly evolving healing practice over the past seven years, and to a limited extent during the previous twenty years, I have used five methods. A few are those most practiced in this country (outside the religious exorcisms of the Catholic Church). All have been effective in removing spirit entities from their positions of attachment with people (or houses, or land), and most are effective with demons (although the shape-shifting variety may be elusive). They are given here in summary form, so readers may have some information regarding what methods are available. Details of these methods are in Appendix C.

Appendix A includes methods for using a pendulum for detecting the presence and number of parasitic spirits and demons. Confidence comes with practice and comparing results with others. Appendix B includes suggestions for additional training that would be helpful for those interested in taking up depossession and exorcism as a healing practice.

On the following pages are summaries of the methods of depossession I have used over the years. Some, such as hypnosis and a medium, are commonly used in America. Others, such as dowsing techniques and shamanic journey, are less used but nonetheless effective. For self-healing work, I recommend the text and script in Chapter Eleven.

Using Dowsing Techniques

This method is for use only in distance work. It provides a high level of protection for the practitioner and is useful for those who are beginning, for those who are afraid or lack confidence to work directly with possessing spirits, and for others who, perhaps due to emergency, need a distance method of exorcism. A working relationship with the pendulum and the archangel Michael is required. After the pendulum has answered some preliminary questions about the client, who is not present, the script of exorcism is read aloud. At the end, the pendulum is used again to check the client to determine whether he or she is clear. Details are presented in Appendix A and C.

Depossession with Hypnosis

Edith Fiore's pioneering works, *The Unquiet Dead* (1987) and *You Have Been Here Before* (1978), provide many case examples and techniques of hypnosis for depossession (and for regression to past lives). As a clinical psychologist and a pioneer in this field of depossession, Fiore presents, in her brief and powerful book, her case experiences and methods of healing illness and addiction due to possessing spirits.

The excellent works of William Baldwin (*Spirit Releasement Therapy*, 1992) and Shakuntala Modi (*Remarkable Healings*, 1997) have expanded Fiore's methods into the realm of depossession of parasitic demons.

Hypnosis is used to assist the client (and the attached being) into a relaxed altered state of consciousness in which the spirit or demon talks with the healer through the voice of the client (client as medium). Again, a working relationship with the archangel Michael for help and protection is essential.

Trained in hypnotherapy, I had no difficulty using Fiore's hypnosis techniques, but during the 1980s and early 90s I was avoiding this work and performed few depossessions. Then, in 1997, as a "guinea pig" in a two-week shamanic healing workshop by the Foundation for Shamanic Studies, I was depossessed of a spirit entity by the leader, Michael Harner, by these, or very similar, methods. That released a block and fired my passion to become more involved in this work.

Depossession with a Medium

A medium is any person who knowingly offers his voice for temporary use by a spirit entity or demon in order for a spirit to be heard and depossession to be performed. Some mediums, through their own will and effort, enter states ranging from light to deep trance. Others function in relatively unaltered states of mind. Usually, the practitioner acts as a negotiator to talk with the spirit entity speaking through the medium. But, as I was told by the shamanic healer-medium who was my partner for three years, there are mediums who perform the roles of both medium and healer-negotiator with the spirit entity.

A medium can be of great assistance in a depossession when he or she has the clairvoyant ability to see a spirit entity and its attachment with a client (its human host), see whether it is releasing from the client or is hesitant and fearful, can assure the spirit entity through thought transfer that there is no trick and no harm will come, see the approach of a possessing spirit entity after it releases from a client, and allow the spirit entity to merge its energy and vibration with the medium's own vocal cords and use the medium's voice.

Face-to-Face Depossession

This work is done with the client acting as the medium through whom the spirit entity or demon speaks to the practitioner. In other words, with the direction of the healer, the client volunteers his or her voice for those that are attached.

The remainder is similar to working with a medium, or even hypnosis as described by Fiore and Baldwin, though the client is not hypnotized in any formal sense. [Note: there are many ways to quickly induce a hypnotic state, such as "the stare" of a person who has a powerful presence, or a sudden sharp voice or handclap. Stage hypnotists are expert at these methods, as are parents, and many successful psychotherapists and shamans use these methods unconsciously].

Clients can perform adequately as mediums if they trust that the experience will not harm them, if they are given time to adjust to the vibrational frequency of the thoughts of the entity or demon, and if the first three to six questions can be answered yes or no, to build confidence that they are receiving and transmitting accurately.

Hearing the entity or demons speak is of dubious benefit to clients, a definite negative to some. They gain some access to the thoughts in the minds of spirit entities, at least to the extent that they care to "peek"; also, the client may understand what it was he did to attract or open a psychic doorway for a possessing spirit or demon. Moreover, the process is a form of proof of possession to the client.

Those who are in training to be "depossessors" or exorcists may find some benefit from knowing why the spirit or demon attached to them, what invitation they hold out to possessing spirits or demons, and what possession feels like in an energetic way.

Shamanic Journey Depossession

The journey to connect with the spirit/soul of the client is conducted in the Middle World, in the here and now of spiritual reality. Possessing spirits and demons are "seen" attached to the client. Suggested methods of dialog and negotiation are presented in the "twelve steps" of depossession in Appendix C.

This method requires basic training in the shamanic journey, and reliable connection with a spirit teacher who agrees to help with the work. Knowledge of the levels and cosmology of the Upper, Middle, and Lower Worlds of spiritual reality, and knowledge of where the soul travels following death, are also very helpful.

Also, I recommend a working connection be made with the archangel Michael, who will help with the removal of the attached spirits and demons, and the archangel Gabriel, who will provide appropriate portals to the light for the various spirit entities. Both archangels will send angelic beings to assist the healer in transporting spirit entities to the portals. It is important to know that a human is required as an intermediary, one who calls on help from the angelic realm, before the angels can become involved with a spirit or person on Earth. The archangel Raphael can be called on as a master of healing, along with the divine light, to provide healing of harm to a person due to possession. The archangel Michael suggested to me that a cross be worn as a form of protection when working with demons.

This chapter has given summaries of several modern practices of depossession. However, it should be clear that none of the methods of depossession is similar to the practices of exorcism modeled by Jesus, as described in Chapter Three.

The following three chapters concern the origin and nature of demons, possession by demons, and the removal of demons that are attached to people.

Chapter Nine

Origin of Demons

The origin of demons in Jewish and Christian stories and traditions is inextricably woven with the origin of Satan and Lucifer. Early rabbinical writings of the Talmud report, in Rudwin's extensive review on the subject (*The Devil In Legend and Literature*, 1973), that when Adam was created on Earth, God told all the angels that they had to bow down because man was greater. But Satan (or Lucifer, or other archangels) rebelled in the company of many other angels, and so God (or the archangel Michael and his angels) cast all of them out of Heaven and down to Earth. Furthermore, the rebellious and earthbound angels were what became the demons. Elaine Pagels (*The Origin Of Satan*, 1995, p. 48–49) recounts a similar origin.

In the Old Testament there is no apparent support for demons having come from angels. Not until Revelations, the last book of the New Testament, said to have been a prophetic and metaphorical channeling from Jesus to an author named John, is the story of the fall of angels recorded in the Bible:

Then there was war in heaven; Michael and the angels under his command fought the Dragon and his [fallen] angels. And the

Dragon lost the battle and was forced out of heaven. This great Dragon — the ancient serpent called the Devil, or Satan, the one deceiving the whole world — was thrown down onto the earth with all his angels (Revelations 12:7–9).

I would call the "Dragon" the leader of the dark forces, the leader of the fallen angels and demons on Earth. His/its "true" name is unknown, just as at present he is unknown because of his great ability to deceive. But that, as will be explained in Chapter Twelve, is changing.

Late in the year 2000, while doing depossession work, I began to sense, in or around some clients, an energy that was counter to what I was doing. It was not open anger, nor was it disapproving in the way of a conscience, but a more disrupting subtle sabotage. Clients who scheduled did not call or show up for a variety of reasons that I had not heard previously: "I forgot," "My car broke down," "I don't have any money." I don't turn away clients from healing for lack of money. I journeyed to my spirit teachers and was advised to study demons, but I didn't know what demons were. Furthermore, I wasn't sure I wanted to know.

Origin of "Lesser" Demons

During Oregon's winter rains that year, I pondered this question and decided the only direct way to find out was the one I tended to avoid: a journey to the center of my dilemma, to find the source and purpose of demons. In preparation for the journey, I called for protection from the archangel Michael and the divine white light of unconditional love. I merged with my spirit teachers, and called for helping animal spirits to join me. Then, calling on Cougar to lead on this adventure, I climbed onto Eagle, and to the rapid beat of a drumming CD, we all flew off to learn about demons.

Eagle flew me down into the deepest level of the shaman's Middle World — what might be thought of as the lower world of the Middle World — to a doorway. I was aware, as in all journeys, that I was enabled to see what ordinarily is invisible to our physical senses and in another dimension of consciousness. Outside the door a small, dull black gargoyle-like creature confronted me and said I couldn't enter. When I asked by whose orders, it said Lucifer's. I challenged it to call Lucifer but it wouldn't. I then told this creature I would remove it with my "light saber." It laughed at the silver metal flashlight handed me by Bear; but when I turned it on, it dissolved in the bright light and its energy transformed into light. (Note: in the Middle World, beyond the veil, in the world of non-ordinary spiritual reality and imagination, dragons, knights and princesses, castles and giants, ogres and little people, devils and demons, anything and everything, is possible — and real.)

Moving to the door again, I was confronted by a fiercer creature, which told me that it was under Lucifer's orders to keep me out and was going to destroy me. As it started toward me, Bear placed a large bowl of water in front of me. I said that I would wash its feet. I think it was surprised and pleased, feeling I was afraid. It placed its feet in the water and instantly began dissolving, just as in the movie *The Wizard of Oz*, when Dorothy "accidentally" dissolved the Wicked Witch of the East by throwing a bucket of water on her.

At the same moment, I was given a vision of John the Baptist in the River Jordan. The people coming to be baptized were covered with black blobs of possessing demons, like leeches on the skin of those crossing a jungle river. When baptized, the demons dissolved in the river and were transformed into pure energy, and the people were washed clean, symbolic of an inner cleansing of the soul. I could not tell whether this vision was metaphoric or literal.

Once through the door, I felt "pulled" to a dark cave in the lowest corner of this part of the Middle World. Upon entering a large room in the cave, everything seemed black, though some kind of reflected light emanated from an unseen source. The floor, ceiling, and walls of the room were composed of or lined with small, dark squirming bodies, like masses of maggots in a long-dead corpse. On individual faces were glaring red eyes and voracious grins.

A single "person," whom I recognized as the spirit entity of a male, stood like a leader in the center of the room. He was paying me no attention, and I didn't know whether to be pleased or affronted. He went on with his business with a dull black, doll-like form, crudely molded to appear human. This was given to him by another human spirit entity that had his head bowed in the manner of a subordinate. As the leader blew into the chest of the small, dark form, a small light, a small spark, appeared in the eyes, and the doll-like form began slowly squirming. Then, he blew his breath into the top of its head, then said a lot of words, and the eyes of the form gleamed as if understanding had been created. As the leader spoke more into the top of the creature's head, its body and face began taking on a terrible, grotesque appearance, grimacing in torment, and a horrible smell swept over the cave. At some level I understood that a demon had been created. This newly formed demon was handed over to the subordinate, who carried it from the room.

The leader turned to me and growled, "You! If you give me any trouble I will destroy you." Not understanding the personal reference, I hurriedly explained that I was there to learn, and not to create trouble. I asked whether he had created everything here. He replied he had. I then asked what they were made of. He said, "Your thoughts." I said, "No way did my thoughts form those!" He laughed a nasty, knowing laugh, and said, "I have followers all over the surface of the Earth, at all times, through all time. Every thought you have about someone produces a thought form that travels to the person you think of. The negative thought forms, because they travel slower than the light ones, are easier to catch. My followers have orders to catch every one they can. Mostly, we get what's left over or splattered around after it hits its target. We do the same with emotions. Back through all of time, there have been periods of great human emotional outpouring. The Inquisition is a treasure chest because of all the millions of women who were killed and all the emotions they released at their deaths. Another is the Holocaust, with its millions of men, women, and children. That is a very rich time, as are all great wars, which are times of major pain and suffering for the common human being. So are times of great famine, and great pestilence, such as the plague in Europe and the influenza epidemic in America. Of course, the purpose of these great events of war, famine, and pestilence is to provide cause for dark despair and terror, to provide reason for separating humans from the Creator, all for the purpose of testing human response to negativity."

Not wanting to break the flow, I neither moved nor spoke. He continued, "The negative thoughts and feelings are collected, then brought here to those who stuff them in a mold where they are pressed and stamped into a much denser form. That form is brought to me. I bring it to life, in a way that I know, and give it a mission — to go out into the world and create chaos and terror;

to shift people from positive to negative emotions toward life; to convert people into forces of the dark."

I asked how he did this. He replied, "Easy. Humans have a dark side, dark capabilities, dark urges that they are unaware of or afraid of, and personalities that are easily addicted. I use the same tools I have used throughout time: drugs, alcohol, and food to numb thought and dull consciousness; sex, money, and power over others to kindle people's greed, lust, and desire for control; tyranny and torture to create oppression and pain; crude, lawless acts to maintain fear; and control of thought and action by possessing demons and spirits, to keep people off balance and out of harmony. All I have to do is get them addicted to their dark side. Testing and temptation have worked worldwide throughout time. A little persistent coaxing or seduction by a demon, with promises that we have no intention or need to keep, is usually enough. Once started, people are easy to keep numb and in a trance where they feel that chasing their material desires is their life's purpose. Grandiosity, vanity, and pride keep them going."

Trying not to think of the depressing implications of what I had just heard, I asked the origin of demons, and he told me they have been here since the beginning. I asked what the beginning was and he said, "The first time a person had a dark thought about himself or someone else, we began production. You have to understand that there wasn't much else going on here at the time. When enough of those thoughts and accompanying negative emotions collected in a slow, dark ball of energy, the form contained various aspects of the minds of those who had thought them into being. And various fragments from the psyches of people who had suffered trauma got caught up in these balls of energy. Enough that these first demons — for that's what they were — had the crude ability to think. We took that as the model for the creation of demons and began the assembly here in these caves."

He glared at me as I started fidgeting at the lengthy explanation, then went on. "We began sending the demons out into the world, to stick to humans, to work their way into holes in their essence. A demon can be an intensifier, like a magnifying mirror, to reflect back the negative beliefs and feelings in the minds of humans. Not only that, but to further intensify the situation in the human mind, the demons add the mix of negative thoughts and emotions they are made of: terror, rage, hate, jealousy, greed, lust, and all the others that grow out of fear. That is enough to get people to start acting out their dark sides, and we would have another victory. And that is really funny, since Lucifer (explained further in Chapter Twelve) is the guardian of the dark side, but he takes the blame for all the chaos the demons create on Earth. We know that he is aware of what we are doing, but he's powerless to touch us because we're part of what humans have chosen to do. We're part of what humans are choosing to do in this moment, and he can't interfere with their free choice. Now, his reputation is so bad, and people are so terrified of the stories we circulate about him, that he will never be a power to help bring people's shadows into the light."

Cautiously, not knowing how much of his talk was the truth, I thanked the leader for the illuminating information, but he was already adding grotesque details to the features of the demonic form in his hands. Before blowing in the dark breath of "life" he asked, "Are you finished here?" The floors, walls, and ceiling began squirming and closing in. Feeling overwhelmed, I nodded affirmatively and we left.

Returning from the journey, I realized that these "lesser" demons have never been human, are not human, and have no souls. Demons are created to support something called the dark forces, and are sent out among people, charged with the task of creating fear and chaos in their lives.

Thus, I began "recognizing" the presence of this type of demon (usually confirmed by pendulum), and doing depossession according to instructions provided by the archangel Michael. I was unaware of anything attached to people that was darker, more negative, or more powerful. My "working" world had definition and I, and my depossessed clients, were happy — until November 2002, that is.

I was doing face-to-face regression work with a client who had a persistent feeling that some deep-rooted darkness lay hidden in his inner being. The suggestion for the regression was that he would return "to the event in this or any other life when something happened that created a deep sense or feeling of negativity."

There was a pause, then a few scattered words in a different voice. I expected to hear about some totally different past life, but the voice took on a sneering, "superior" quality, telling me that I didn't know what I was getting into. Then the client's face slowly began contorting into a grimace, his body curling into a hunched form on hands and knees (we had been sitting on the floor), and the voice deepened to a low growl. I immediately asked the Mighty Warriors of Light to put a bubble filled with light around this demon, and pull it tight so it could not move. That immobilized it, but didn't still the voice. I asked its purpose and it replied, "Kill you." Although the hairs on my back and back of neck were standing straight out, I was feeling no deep concern. Very slowly, the left index finger began moving along the floor toward me, as if poking through the invisible bubble. Then the left shoulder and head began a low movement toward me. I called for the Mighty Warriors to remove the demon, but there was no change. I loudly said, "Stop." It slowed for a moment, then roared, "No." Then the demon lunged at me. I caught the arms by the biceps and could feel an extreme power, considerably stronger than I thought I could restrain. Also, it was partially above me, while I was sitting cross-legged, a poor defensive posture. I called to the archangel Michael to help me remove the demon. At the same instant I became aware that I was holding the demon away from me, and unafraid. Then, in a move that seemed in no way unnatural, or supernatural, I twisted its upper body and forced it face down on the floor, at the same time loudly commanding, "Let it go!" using the client's name. I asked the archangel Michael to remove the demon to where it could cause no further harm. The client's body went limp and slowly relaxed. After he regained some "normalcy," we talked about the experience, which had been startling to both of us. I referred to the demon as a "super-demon." I felt a little ridiculous doing so, but I acknowledged that whatever had been removed was not one of the "lesser" demons I had been "casting out" over the past two years.

Later, in a journey to my spirit teacher, I found that this was a "lesson" to take me to another level of my work. I was told to "upgrade" my practices and, with these "giant demons," to use a "super" bubble filled with light rather than the usual bubble; use the Mighty Warriors of Light on Earth rather than the Mighty Warriors of Light; and call on the archangel Uriel in addition to the archangel Michael.

Origin of Giant Demons and Fallen Angels

With perfect timing, Elizabeth Clare Prophet's book *Fallen Angels: And The Origins of Evil* (2000, p. 104–106) answered my questions about what I was dealing with.

Prophet's intention was to use The Book of Enoch and The Book of Jubilees, apparently written between the times of the Old and New Testaments, but not included in the Bible, to document and prove that the fallen angels, known as "Watchers," and their "progeny," who were said to have been cast out of Heaven by Michael, " … have been on Earth continually since then." She declared, "Therefore, I am prepared to prove and document that they are with us today in positions of power in church and state as prime movers in matters of war and finance…" (p. 5). Prophet republished The Book of Enoch and excerpts from The Book of Jubilees to support her work. I present selected quotations from both to substantiate the origin of what I am calling "giant demons" and "fallen angels":

It happened after the sons of men had multiplied in those days, that daughters were born to them, elegant and beautiful. And when the angels, the sons of Heaven [the Watchers, in the Aramaic text], beheld them, they became enamoured of them, saying to each other, Come, let us select for ourselves wives from the progeny of men, and let us beget children. Then their leader Samyaza [Semihazah, in Aramaic] said to them, I fear that you may perhaps be indisposed to the performance of this enterprise; and that I alone shall suffer for so grievous a crime. But they answered him and said, We all swear, and bind ourselves by mutual execrations, that we will not change our intention, but execute our projected undertaking. Then they swore all together, and all bound themselves by mutual execrations. Their whole number was two hundred, who descended upon Ardis, which is the top of Mount Armon. (Enoch 7:1–7.)

Then they took wives, each choosing for himself, whom they began to approach, and with whom they cohabited; teaching them sorcery, incantations, and the dividing of roots and trees.

And the women conceiving brought forth giants, whose stature was each three hundred cubits. These devoured all that the labor of men produced, until it became impossible to feed them; when they turned themselves against men, in order to devour them; and began to injure birds, beasts, reptiles, and fishes, to eat their flesh one after another (or one another's flesh), and to drink their blood. (Enoch 7:10–14.)

This provides clearer meaning as to why, without any preamble, the following four verses were inserted in abridged fashion into the history of Noah's life in Genesis, as an explanation of the "wickedness of man," to provide God's "rationale" for the flood to wipe out "everyone" on Earth.

When the human population began to grow rapidly on the earth, the sons of God [Elohim–Hebrew, angels]saw the beautiful women of the human race and took any they wanted as their wives. In those days, and even afterward, when the evil beings from the spirit world were sexually involved with human women, their children became giants, of whom so many legends are told. (Genesis 6:1–4.)

Verse four, which begins with "In those days" begins in the Hebrew text with "Ha-Npiliym" and is translated in the Revised Standard Version and several others as:

> The Nephilim were on the earth in those days, and also afterward. (Genesis 6:4.)

In the King James Version, Nephilim was translated as "giants," which seems a strange mistranslation. I believe, as shown by Zechariah Sitchin's research (*Divine Encounters*, 1995, p.73), that the Nephilim were extraterrestrials descended from the Anunnaki. The Bible (Num. 13:33) explains that the Nephilim were the "sons of Anak" (Hebrew for the Anunakki, in Sumerian "Those who from heaven to earth came").

Another piece is needed from The Book of Jubilees to complete the picture of the origin of giant demons (Jubilees V:1–8).

> And it came to pass when the children of men began to multiply on the face of the earth and daughters were born unto them, that the angels of God saw them on a certain year of this jubilee, that they were beautiful to look upon; and they took themselves wives of all whom they chose, and they bare unto them sons and they were giants [emphasis mine].
>
> And lawlessness increased on the earth and all flesh corrupted its way, alike men and cattle and beasts and birds and everything that walketh on the earth — all of them corrupted their ways and their orders, and they began to devour each other, and lawlessness increased on the earth and every imagination of the thoughts of all men [was] thus evil continually. And God looked upon the earth, and behold it was corrupt, and all flesh had corrupted its orders, and all that were upon the earth had

wrought all manner of evil before his eyes. And He said, I shall destroy man and all flesh upon the face of the earth which I have created. But Noah found grace before the eyes of the Lord.

And against *the angels whom He had sent upon the earth* [emphasis mine], He was exceedingly wroth, and He gave commandments to root them out of all their dominions, and He bade us [the archangels] to bind them in the depths of the earth, and behold they are bound in the midst of them, and are (kept) separate. And against their sons went forth a command from before His face that they should be smitten with the sword, and be removed from under heaven.

In the caves of Qumran, fragments of scrolls were found that have been called "The Book of Giants" (*The Dead Sea Scrolls*, Wise, et al, 1996). One of those fragments speaks of the origin and nature of the giants:

4Q531 Frag. 2 [...] they defiled [...[...they begot] giants and monsters [...] they begot, and, behold, all [the earth was corrupted...] [...] with its blood and by the hand of [...] [giants] which did not suffice for them and [...] and they were seeking to devour many [...] the monsters attacked it (pp. 247–48).

The "monsters" are nowhere else explained unless they are the offspring of breeding experiments by the Nephilim.

In Enoch, God speaks directly to Enoch, explaining the nature of the giants:

Now the giants, who have been born of spirit and of flesh, shall be called upon earth evil spirits, and on earth shall be their habitation. Evil spirits shall proceed from their flesh, because they were created from above, from the holy. Watchers was their beginning and their primary foundation. Evil spirits shall they be upon earth, and the spirits of the wicked shall they be called. The habitation of the spirits of heaven shall be in heaven; but upon earth shall be the habitation of terrestrial spirits, who are born on earth. (Enoch 15:8.) [Emphasis mine.]

In The Book of Jubilees, Noah spoke to his sons about the historical reasons for the "flood," indicating that in the past there were four forms of physical life on earth warring with one another: the giants, the Nephilim, the Eljo (something of God), and mankind. The Watchers too were present:

[Noah speaks] For owing to these three things came the flood upon the earth, namely, owing to the fornication wherein the Watchers against the law of their ordinances went a whoring after the daughters of men, and took themselves wives of all which they chose: and they made the beginning of uncleanness. (Jubilees VII: 21.)

And they begat sons the Naphidim, and they were all unlike [said to be "corrupt" text by Prophet. I understand it to mean the Nephilim were performing breeding experiments with various life forms such that the offspring all were unlike], and they devoured one another: and the giants slew the Naphil, and the Naphil slew the Eljo, and the Eljo mankind, and one man another. And every one sold himself to work iniquity and to shed much blood, and the earth was filled with iniquity. And after this they sinned against the beasts and birds, and all that moveth and walketh on the earth: and much blood was shed on the earth, and every imagination and desire of men imagined vanity and evil continually. (Jubilees VII: 22–24.) [Emphasis mine.]

Later, as Noah's sons' sons were experiencing troubles typical of the "seductions" of demonic possession, lust, addictions, and murder, which had the intention of destroying them, Noah prayed to God to imprison the demons, to not let them rule or have power over the "spirits of the living" because, "Thou alone canst exercise dominion over them" (Jubilees X:6). The archangel Michael is the apparent speaker recounting what happened:

> And the chief of the spirits, Mastema [from the Hebrew verb mastim, to be adverse, equivalent to Satan, the Adversary], came and said, "Lord, Creator, let some of them remain before me, and let them hearken to my voice, and do all that I shall say unto them; for if some of them are not left to me, I shall not be able to execute the power of my will on the sons of men; for these are for corruption and leading astray before my judgment, for great is the wickedness of the sons of men." And He [Lord] said, "Let the tenth part of them remain before him, and let nine parts descend into the place of condemnation." (Jubilees X:8–9.)

> And one of us [the archangel Raphael according to Prophet's footnote 7, per Hebrew Book of Noah] He commanded that we should teach Noah all their medicines; for He knew that they would not walk in uprightness, nor strive in righteousness. And we did [Michael and the angels] according to His words: all the malignant evil ones we bound in the place of condemnation, and a tenth part of them we left that they might be subject before Satan [Mastemah?] on the earth. And we explained to Noah all the medicines of their diseases, together with their seductions, how he might heal them with herbs of the earth. And Noah wrote down all things in a book as we instructed him concerning

every kind of medicine. Thus the evil spirits were precluded from hurting the sons of Noah. (Jubilees X:10–13.)

I understand from my spirit teacher that "a tenth part" is a very large number, more than I could imagine. But these, according to The Book of Enoch, were to have been confined before the flood, or destroyed by the flood, so why are they still present, and in such large numbers? I am told that — as a mystery — at each of the times of apparent destruction, some, many, or all of the fallen angels, the leaders of the rebellion, and their giant-demon offspring, went to safe havens, both of earth and not earth, where they remained until the timing was right and safe for their return.

But fallen angels still are present, though the ones remaining on Earth, according to my spirit teacher, are invisible and discarnate, and mostly attached to human hosts. Most are inactive, but some are active. Their leadership apparently is in another realm. They have the nature and powers of angels, but their intent is rebellious, to control Earth, and not necessarily for the highest good of humans.

God mandated in the Book of Enoch (Enoch 15:8) that the giants were to be called evil spirits. Later they were called demons. I am calling them "giant demons." Their intent, as I understand it, is to steal the power of selected humans, slowly, over time, stealing their "light," their upper soul. Incrementally, the possessed person would sink deeper and deeper into his dark side, his shadow self, or lower soul. The giant demons offer temptations of material riches and powers in trade for souls, as they did to Jesus. They battle for control of the Earth in a war between those of light and those of darkness, as recorded by many cultures and religions, e.g., the War Scroll of the Essenes,

Zoroaster's story in Persia, and the Bhagavad Gita of India.

The "flood" in the Near East, recorded in Sumerian and Hebrew histories, was said in the Bible and the Book of Enoch to be for the purpose of wiping the slate clean of the iniquity and wickedness of humans, fallen angels, and giant demons. However, some, many, or all of these moved, or were moved, from the area of the flood and awaited a new time, the time of Noah's sons' sons, to come back to the area and continue their appointed path.

Present Fallen Angels

The fallen angels are those who were sent to Earth by God "in the beginning" as Watchers, watching over the early ventures of humans. As such, they felt that Earth was "their" domain. They became seduced by the beauty of women, which caused them to rebel against God's orders to the extent that they physically cohabited with women. In this, they did not "fall," unless it was to fall out of favor with God. The unions resulted in the demigods that grew into giants. Although the fallen angels had the attributes of angels, they were not above acting like giant demons to gain their ends. While not demons or evil spirits, they could manipulate and seduce the demons and giant demons to do their bidding for a time, until the giant demons grew out of their control.

At that time, the fallen angels appear to have withdrawn from physical presence on Earth to a nearby dimension. There may have been a split within the fallen angels. There are those who could see, in the abilities of their giant-demon offspring, ways to prevent humans intent on being "lightworkers" from achieving personal power. However, there appear to be other fallen angels who were hurt by the destruction caused by the demonic offspring and their inability to change them.

The intent of fallen angels has been wide ranging over time, possibly as a reflection of dominant human intentions, sometimes peaceful and sometimes dark, but generally to "rule" over Earth. Because they cannot overrule free will, given as a law of Earth, they can only manipulate and magnify what is there. If a person's desire is power, they can seduce the person to their ends with all the skills of a Madison Avenue advertising corporation. They are the origin of sex in advertising.

Present Giant Demons

Giant demons are the offspring resulting from the union of incarnate angels and humans, and the descendants of those unions. Being mixed with human ego, they are demigods and much different and more complex than angels. Their intent is the destruction of the light side of humanity. They are not constrained by moral concepts of "highest good." It is not clear whether they are under the control of "divine providence." Similar to the demigods of Babylonian, Trojan, Grecian, Hindu, Roman, and Norse "myths," they have no compunction about killing and wars. They are "The Adversary." Their favored method of supporting the dark forces is to attach parasitically to hosts who are either "darkworkers," who desire power over others and are willing to trade their souls and support the dark forces for it, or "lightworkers" who show, by the colors and brightness of their auras, that if they come into personal power in service of humanity, they will threaten the goals of the giant demons and dark forces.

The New Spirituality

The fallen angels and giant demons originate in the mists of ancient mythology. They come from a time of mass fear of the awesome and unknown powers and forces of the universe. People were searching for any answers that made sense of their existence.

In the new spirituality, we will not "have" to create the presence in our lives of fearsome beings such as fallen angels and demons, which flourish in a state of being of "I am afraid" or "I am judgment." People living in those states of being would attract fear-provoking events or people into their lives, whereas individuals choosing a state of being such as "I am love" or "I am strong and whole" would attract entirely different events and people.

Chapter Ten

Possession by Demons

Symptoms of Possession

Possession by demons is usually felt much more distinctly than the presence of parasitic spirit entities. However, outward signs of the demon, as a physical entity, will not show until the demon "comes out" of hiding. As long as a demon is not challenged or called out, as is common in religious exorcism, all evidence is indirect and provided by actions of the people carrying the demon, who usually feel some or most of the following:

- Continually tired or exhausted
- A pervading sense or fear that something bad is going to happen
- A sense of lack of control in their lives
- Their lives, for unknown reasons, are falling apart, being destroyed
- Driven to do terrible things, things that they may know are "wrong" (tell lies, spread gossip, suddenly leave family or job, hurt their children or pets, hurt themselves, kill something, someone, or themselves)
- "Ordered" by an internal or external voice from "God,"

"Satan," or "an angel" to do the above actions, and/or feel that such actions are "right"
- Are internally counseled to miss appointments for therapy, "healing," or medical needs

People with well-developed willpower and ego boundaries may feel early symptoms at a very subtle level, such that they seem insignificant. These may grow slowly with time and may not attain the maximum intensities indicated above.

People who lack personal power, whose egos are poorly developed, who harbor hidden fears about life and themselves, who are filled with prejudices about people and religion, etc., or who hold delusions of themselves as being "bad," might begin at more intense levels. Some of these people may have experienced emotional instability or mental health issues, and may have undergone psychiatric evaluation and/or care at some time, particularly when alcohol or drugs are involved.

The physical signs of the giant demon, like deer tracks in new-fallen snow, are easily read and understood, even by a first-time viewer. The following are seen and heard when the demon comes into view:
- The person's face contorts to an unnatural and "ugly" grimace that provokes an instant reaction of fear and desire to be elsewhere in the onlooker.
- Eyes show flashes of red, as of microbursts of rage.
- The voice becomes deep, hoarse, unpleasant, demanding, sneering, or seducing. The change is most noticed in women, but unmistakable in men. At times the voice consists solely of hissing and spitting, like a high-voltage line in wet grass.
- Shoulders become hunched, the neck disappears into them, and the entire upper body appears to be larger and stronger.

- If the demon is threatened, the conversation may become filled with violent threats of what the demon will do.

These physical signs indicate that the demon has varying control of the nervous system, voice, and musculature. Fully provoked demons, such as commonly occurs during religious exorcisms, may require several adults to constrain them.

Oesterreich (*Possession*, 1966) reviewed historical literature for signs of possession from the times of Jesus to the 1800s (p. 17–25). He found that some of those possessed were shaken by their demons, some thrown to the ground, and some became extremely ("supernaturally") strong. Others apparently had no violent tendencies. Oesterreich reported that the absence of violence might indicate possession by a spirit entity rather than a demon.

In *Entity Possession: Freeing the energy body of negative influences* (1997), Samuel Sagan combines an understanding of Taoist and esoteric perspectives of subtle energy bodies and entities. In his definition, an entity is any presence that can parasitize human beings (p. 1). Sagan claims, "In 99 percent of all cases, an entity could never be called evil. It is just an energy in the wrong place" (p. 146). However, he presents several case studies representing the remaining 1 percent. I would characterize them as typical of demons.

One of his women clients picked up entities during a vacation that included illicit sex. From her view, the demons told her to be promiscuous; they enjoyed her having intercourse, and could arouse her to have sex with them at night. This is an example of an incubus, or male sex demon, a succubus being the female demon that demands sex at night from men.

A male client, on holiday in Thailand, was visited by an evil spirit that promised him eternal life. He felt that it was a lie, that it represented eternal death. The man became very agitated, was unable to sleep, and could read people's minds and see nonphysical beings. Twice he tried to commit suicide. He reported the entity wanted his spirit so he could possess and control it.

William Baldwin's book, *Spirit Releasement Therapy* (1995), is a scholarly compendium of his clinical experiences with depossession, which he has trademarked as "spirit releasement." His case studies are of both discarnate spirit entities and demons. Following the path of Edith Fiore, his former teacher, his book also treats of regression and past-life therapy. In addition, it differentiates between possession and multiple personality disorders (MPD). His method of spirit releasement is hypnosis, using dialog (through the client) with possessing spirits and demons.

Baldwin indicated that demons thrive on human pain, can induce violence that can lead to murder, and can so undermine the value of one with low self-esteem as to cause suicide. He reported that they appear to him as black shapes within the structure of a person's aura, and to his clients as dark birds or glaring gargoyles (p. 282).

Demons as "Drivers"

Demons, particularly the "giant" demons described later, are drivers of people's behaviors. From comments gathered from clients and literature, people are "driven":

- To have troubles/drama with relationships, jobs, money, deciding "what to do" with their lives
- To hurt (through violence or some form of verbal, physical, or sexual tyranny) spouse, children, a neighbor, or the stranger on the next bar stool

- To run away from the life they have built to that point in time (from job, family, commitment or responsibility, or future)
- To seek revenge for perceived or fantasized wrongs
- To lie, cheat, and steal
- To kill (self or others)

In psychological literature, all of these drives might be classified as obsessions or compulsions. An obsession is the dominating action or influence of a persistent idea that the individual cannot escape. So, what appears on the surface as obsession may have possession, behind the scenes, as its root cause. Psychotherapists have referred a number of "obsessive-compulsive" clients to me; invariably, each has had a parasitic demon. The psychotherapy was reported to progress "more effectively and faster" following my removal of the demons.

Doorways for Demons

I have found that a person must first open some personal "doorway" that invites a demon before it can "come in" and attach. When no doorway is present, demons may be nearby but lack a point of entry to the energetic body. Doorways through which I have found demons able to enter people:

- Negative thoughts about others (commonly denied), or malicious gossip about others
- Negative and disparaging thoughts about oneself
- Drugs and alcohol, whether for recreation, socially acceptable suicide, or to numb reality
- Emotional outbursts of hatred, rage, terror, or revenge, targeted at someone or something
- Other fear-based emotions (such as feeling sad, "bad," or

worthless as regards self or life)

- Feeling pity or sorry for another, a subtle judgment of "I'm okay, you're not"
- Vanity and other ego-based pride that elevates a person in his mind over others
- Religious, racial, class, or other organizational fanaticism
- Personal judgments of others regarding race, social class, sex, appearance, or other
- Lust for power over people in terms of control, sex, or money

Habitual or obsessive practices, such as the above listed "doorways," must change following depossession or exorcism or demons will return.

Possession by Demons

Demons have always used fear and seduction to gain their way with humans. In the biblical Garden of Eden, Eve was seduced into eating fruit from the "tree of knowledge of good and evil" by what I have been informed was a shape-shifting giant demon in the form of a serpent. Most tribal cultures revere snakes and dragons for their great spiritual powers of transformation. And throughout mythology, the snake has been the ally and power helper of the goddess. Little wonder, then, that Eve followed the serpent's advice to sample the fruit of the tree. Eve reported to God, "The serpent beguiled me...." (Genesis 3:13)

Each individual has a unique weakness in his personal armor that causes him to be enchanted by a particular form of seduction over all others. Some men feel they "lose their heads" or give up their power with women who have a certain look, voice, touch, or smell. A friend of mine once told me that he became "like putty" when a woman would lay her hand on his arm. Some women are attracted to or feel "driven" to meet — even though they intuit where the path will lead — the one man, in a room full of men, who will be their source of pain and misery.

Possessing "lesser" demons operate with human beings in three ways:

- Attached on their own within the person's energetic body;
- Attached piggyback to an attached spirit entity; or
- As shape-shifters, free to move about throughout the physical and energetic body and mind, in whatever form they choose.

Like magnifying mirrors, all three forms act as intensifiers of fears and beliefs within the possessed person's mind, but also add to the mix the foreign negative thought forms and intense emotions they are made of. Giant demons usually operate singly. They have greater ability and processes for thinking than the "lesser" demons, and are more aware that they are part of a battle for control of humanity.

The process of parasitization by demons usually is one of escalation, starting small, barely noticeable, and growing to a condition that becomes obvious within and sometimes outside the host. The simplest condition is one where a single emotion that the possessed person holds, such as fear, is intensified or magnified over time until the feeling consumes the person's entire existence. That person may become house bound, a bedridden shut-in, totally afraid to step outside. Children may become terrified of entering a dark bedroom, where they believe that demons and spirits are waiting.

As the symptoms of demonic presence escalate, the strength of character of the host's personality may also change in an attempt to keep behaviors within the boundaries of social acceptance. A client who spent many years drinking in bars gave me an example: as the night wore on, and the alcohol would begin to erode his social boundaries, his language would coarsen, and he would approach women even if they were with other men. When he first began drinking, he would commonly get into fights. As the years went on, he learned to back off from a fight and buy everyone a drink. He thought he was becoming wiser; in actuality, he was developing habits that would camouflage the demon.

I have had my own experiences with demons. Not long ago, a friend walked into the room where I was working, looking haggard and exhausted in contrast to her usual bright energy. I felt a sudden expansion of my heart in sympathy for whatever was going on. She described her phone call with a friend and how she had felt distressed over her friend's health troubles. As she talked, I slowly began to feel irritated at her interruption of my work. Then, as she began describing her feelings of sympathy for her friend, I felt like a fire had ignited in my belly, small at first, but inexorably fed by a fuel that was out of my control. I felt myself glaring as if my eyes alone could control her and make her stop talking. I realized I was becoming enraged, a wild, hot feeling I hadn't experienced in many years. She asked me what was happening and I replied that I thought I had a demon. Using methods of exorcism I had taught her, she removed it. My relief was instantaneous. The fire of my rage died away to nothing but a memory. I wrote myself a memo to do some inner work on the agreement to not take things personally, and on the difference between sympathy and compassion (the knowledge that what people experience is through choices they have made). As we reviewed the episode, we realized that she had felt sympathy for her friend, thereby opening a doorway for the shape-shifting demon that had been attached to the friend, and through the phone wires transferred it to herself. In turn, in sympathy for the unusual expression on her face, I had transferred it to me — a very complex healing for the three of us.

Shape-shifting Demons

During my early experience of shamanic journeys to clients, I encountered some demons that seemed to be very elusive and to move around within the body. I journeyed to the archangel Michael to ask about what I was seeing. He told me, "Demons can shape-shift into the form of rats and many other forms. They may be hidden inside the energetic body of a client and be invisible and undetectable until the healer has been totally healed of possession, and all 'critical' soul fragments are returned by shamanic soul retrieval. This may include fragments lost during the 'original' trauma of separation from God in the beginning." Michael's second sentence clarifies why many healers are unable to detect spirit entities and/or demons in clients who come to them for help. I did not understand the sentence until I found later that I had experienced soul loss when separating from God at the time of my first incarnation.

The shape-shifting demon is the most elusive and difficult to define, and is therefore perhaps the most dangerous, except for the giant demons and fallen angels. Shape-shifting demons appear to move to the organ or place in the body where the person's most negative core beliefs about self are focused. I have seen them (shamanically) in the legs, groin, sex organs, belly, chest, heart, throat, jaws, and head. Within a human body they appear to be able to simulate physical symptoms such as aches, pains, and swelling. Some clients report feeling a clutching or closing of the throat, others a grabbing sensation in the belly, and some a sharp pain in the heart. They have been seen as rats, bats, blobs of slime, magicians, and various forms of spirit guide. They can appear as spiritual friends, their voices soothing and kind to the possessed person, even while suggesting that the person harm himself or someone else "for your highest good."

But most often, shape-shifting demons feel anything but beneficial. For example, until she learned new "habits," a therapist called me several times during a three-month period, fearful of a heart attack, her pulse rate very high, and a choking sensation in her throat. Each time I would find a shape-shifting demon firmly locked in her throat, attempting energetically to choke her (into submission to stop her work). Like a psychic vacuum cleaner, she had removed the demon from a client through her highly sensitive and empathic nature. Infuriated with her interference with its mission, the demon would jump down her throat (in the subtle energy of her etheric body, with sensory overflow to her physical body), which was her most vulnerable body part due to her dependence on her voice in her work. The threat of losing her voice would make internal fears escalate rapidly into terror, resulting in a panic attack. Removal of the demon would erase all signs of panic within a minute or two.

The Watchers

The "lesser" demons seem to be monitored continuously by watcher demons. With shamanic vision, I have viewed them perched in trees, on telephone poles, and hanging from roof gutters on buildings, much like the gargoyles that imitate them. Somewhere around the watcher there is usually a "watcher of the watcher" that is in contact with the network of demons from the Earth's surface down to the deep cavern where demons are formed.

When watchers are not removed along with the possessing demons, another demon will likely be sent. If a person has been healed, for example, by shamanic soul retrieval and energetic reweaving of the auric grid of the subtle energy body, and there is no opening for entry, a demon may wait in the person's periphery for a new emotional or judgmental "doorway" to open. When the watchers are removed, the link between the person and the demons is broken.

Fallen Angels

Fallen angels, although angels originally, are demonic in practice since their split with God. They carry out their intent to rule over Earth through possession of humans, all female in my experience, who would grow to have sufficient personal power to challenge their authority. Fallen angels may seduce a woman into powerlessness by inducing her to develop some debilitating illness, or to single-mindedly pursue a joyless job, with hopes focused on retirement, despite being aware that her spiritual life's purpose is to engage in other work of service to people. And, through fears of what might happen if she ventures outdoors, a woman may remain "house-bound."

Fallen angels have been known to masquerade as helping angels. I worked with a client who was convinced that what I was describing as a fallen angel was her guardian angel and had been sent to her by God. She was unwilling to have it removed, despite hearing its intention, in dialog with me, "to protect and control her." As I slept that night, I felt like I was leaving my body as in astral travel. Then I became aware that many small black demons were being directed by an angel to steal my soul from my body. Instinctively, I "knew" that the angel was the fallen angel from the woman of the day before and that the purpose of the attack was to render me powerless. In dream time the angel appeared very tall and shadowy, a dark form with wings that enfolded the demons and me. With my will, I pulled my soul from their hands and called for the archangel Michael to help and protect me. They vanished as he appeared with his sword flashing blue light. I slept peacefully the remainder of the night. The following day, the client indicated that she had been tormented by something during the night that had seemed to her to be the fallen angel. She wanted it removed, which was done, and no further problems occurred.

The following dialog with a fallen angel is through a fifty-six-year old woman client who had been disabled and bedridden for eleven years. For twenty-one years before that, mental health issues had kept her dependent on others for her care.

John: What do you call yourself?

FA: "Proxy." I'm deceitful.

John: How many years have you been with her in this life?

FA: Thirty-two.

John: What was your purpose with her?

FA: Block her knowledge, keep her ignorant.

John: And how did you do that?

FA: Kept her separated from people and books. But it didn't work.

John: What happened?

FA: She broke through. She got information. We did not understand the computer and the Internet.

John: Then what did you do?

FA: I knocked her down. She fell physically. That was when she was put to bed [became "bedridden"]

John: What has changed since then?

FA: She got over her panic disorder. She knows too much. You confuse things.

John: Have you known her before in other lives?

FA: Oh yes. For hundreds of thousands of years. When she was commissioned to Orion. Then when she was sent here to start human life.

John: Do you stay with her following death?

FA: No. When she dies we can't go to the light. We have to wait for her return.

John: How can you tell it's her?

FA: We see her. There's a special vibration to her light. I know her vibration.

John: Would you like the opportunity to be reconnected with God?

FA: Yes.

The archangels Michael and Uriel took the fallen angel to the "place of confinement" underneath the Earth, known by Michael from a directive by God (Enoch 10:15) and then to the "womb of transformation" (a large human-shaped crystal named by Crystal Dawn Morris, Occidental, California, 2002), in which fallen angels (and giant demons) are dismembered by crystalline light and returned to God's judgment.

In dialog with fallen angels through clients, they have told me that their present form is both incarnate and discarnate, so they are not limited to being in possession of humans to have a physical existence. Their present location is both on Earth and in some nearby realm that they created. They have organizational structure and leadership.

In the definition of "exorcism" from the *Catholic Encyclopedia* (2003) exists an interesting reference to fallen angels (and demons):

According to Catholic belief demons or fallen angels retain their natural power, as intelligent beings, of acting on the material universe, and using material objects and directing material forces for their own wicked ends; and this power, which is in itself limited, and is subject, of course, to the control of divine providence, is believed to have been allowed a wider scope for its activity in the consequence of the sin of mankind. Hence places and things as well as persons are naturally liable to diabolical infestation, within limits permitted by God, and exorcism in regard to them is nothing more than a prayer to God, in the name of His Church, to restrain this diabolical power supernaturally, and a profession of faith in His willingness to do so on behalf of his servants on Earth.

The only "limit" to the power of fallen angels appears to be the outright killing of their hosts, as in the story of Job in the Old Testament. However, the "control of divine providence" appears to allow them to destroy everything else in a person's life, as was done to Job. The presence of hundreds of serial and mass killers in this country testifies to the truth that fallen angels and especially giant demons, if not permitted to actually squeeze a trigger, are capable of driving their host to murder. And even though "divine providence" may restrain demons from killings, many suicides appear to have demonic possession at the root.

Giant Demons

Following the "flood," said in the Book of Enoch to have been created to destroy everything evil in the Earth (En. 10:4), the surviving giant demons (and fallen angels) disappeared from Earth by becoming discarnate and invisible. They maintain their presence and intent to control the Earth for the dark forces by parasitically attaching with humans that are perceived as threats. In shamanic vision, they have appeared to me as huge, dark energetic forms towering over and wrapped around the human with whom they are attached. To the one with whom they are attached, giant demons have the ability to shape-shift into the perceived form and voice of "God" or "Satan" and many other forms that test, tempt, seduce, or demand people to do their bidding.

Their intent is to select humans who have the potential for becoming powerful lightworkers (for definition see www.lightworker.com) on Earth at some time, even in the distant future, and keep them weak by stealing their power, their "light," the energy of their upper souls. This may have already have happened during several lifetimes in the past. The easiest time for stealing or trading for a human soul has always been the time before death, at which time some people may be willing to give their souls to forestall what they mistakenly believe to be the painful finality of death. But in the workings of karma, the person who dies disempowered in one life will come back in another to face similar challenges of lack of power.

Some people may despair of ever gaining personal power; others may have a strong desire for power over others. Either may accept the tempting offers of demons, as the dark forces are willing to promise anything, especially as they have no intent or need to keep their promises. Then, the people become trapped as part of the forces of darkness, and can allow the urges of their dark sides to get out of control. Major examples of this behavior are historic figures such as Hitler, Stalin, Pol Pot, and Genghis Khan, who each created a kingdom of tyranny over the people they ruled.

I offer the following two dialogs with giant demons through the voices of clients to illustrate the nature, tactics, and purpose of the giant demons. The first is a highly intuitive thirty-nine-year-old who is having trouble getting his life started. He recently had broken off a relationship with a woman who appears to have been a sorceress in her past life and a portal for the dark forces in this life. When he feels her thinking of him, desiring him back, and thinks of the love they had and lost, he feels like he is two years old again. He becomes hurt and afraid, then angry, which opens his doorway for a giant demon to enter.

John: Tell me your name.

GD: Russell [the name appears to be "picked" from the mind of the host].

John: Where did you come from?

GD: I came from a dark place, from the others.

John: Why to him (by name)?

GD: I was summoned to him specifically.

John: What is your purpose with him?

GD: To stop his progress, his work, his productivity.

John: What's special about him?

GD: He's a "lightworker" … spreads his light to others.

John: What did he do that allowed you to attack?

GD: He gets angry and hurt about losing her, and he asks to die.

John: Then what is your intent?

GD: To help him get what he asks for — death.

The giant demon was removed to the "place of confinement" and "womb of transformation." Apparently, the client, during a time of anguish a week previous, had said aloud, "If my life isn't going to get better, I'd rather be dead." The point is, "Be careful what you ask for!"

The following example is of a thirty-one-year-old woman with psychic abilities. She began her phone call to me by saying, "I awoke this morning from a sound sleep to this demon sitting on my chest and choking me. I could see and feel it. When I cried out, it left." She agreed to "lend" her voice to the demon so I could dialog with it:

John: How long have you been with her?

GD: Since B.C.

John: What is B.C.?

GD: One thousand B.C. Many years.

John: During how many lifetimes?

GD: Three lifetimes. Others have been other times.

John: What is your intent with her?

GD: Destruction! To finish her ability as a seer. To finish her getting her power.

John: What's your purpose for that? What does it accomplish?

GD: Gain power — take their light for my power.

John: What would that accomplish?

GD: More power — more darkness.

John: And what do you look like?

GD: We have four legs. We crawl, we can jump. We can hide from you, under things, in dark corners.

John: How would I recognize you?

GD: Can change appearances … for a few minutes … to a man.

John: Then what can you do?

GD: Stand between them. [The reply became unclear, and the demon became agitated. It said something like "interfere in her relationships with men."]

The shape-shifting giant demon was removed. When I called her the next morning, the client told me she felt highly energetic, and her house, which had been haunted by a demon that was also removed at the same time, felt really great to her. "And," she said, "I feel as if I'm in a kind of swirling energy of light."

The giant demons are human adversaries. I was told during a journey that giant demons were "The Adversary" (Hebrew for Sa-tan) in most biblical stories: first as reptile in the story of Eve and Adam in the Garden; several thousand years later, with Jesus in the desert; with Judas, who betrayed Jesus for promises of money; and with the power-driven Romans and Jews who presided over the trials that led to Jesus' death.

Demons and Illness

Demons were often seen as the source of illness. In Old Testament times they were given names related to the illness with which they were associated (*Illustrated Dictionary and Concordance of The Bible*, 1986). *Keteb*, translated as "sudden death" (Deuteronomy 32:24; Hosea 13:14), was the bringer of a deadly plague and a messenger of Sheol (Hades, from Greek; Land of the Dead in the Lower World). *Reshef* was a god of plague in Mesopotamia, possibly the Fever demon (Psalms 78: 49). *Azazel* was a demon that lived in the wilderness, to some a former archangel, to me a fallen angel, sometimes called scapegoat (Leviticus 16:8, 10, 26), on whose head at Atonement were placed the community's misdeeds before it was banished into the wilderness. *Lilith*, called "night creature" (Isaiah 34:14), was the name of a female demon of Mesopotamia and Israel who tempted men sexually; the first may have been Adam in the Garden. *Dever*, translated as "pestilence," along with *Reshef*, was seen with God as he was about to pronounce judgment on Earth (Habakkuk 3:5).

According to Rudwin (p. 24), Jews at the time of Jesus still believed that demons were the source of diseases such as asthma, croup, hydrophobia, insanity, and indigestion. He cites sources that indicate that the naming practice, and the belief, may have come from neighboring Assyrians. Whether healing of those illnesses was done by exorcism of demons before the time of Jesus is not reported in the Bible.

In our present culture, where greater health conditions and longevity occur than in ancient Israel, I believe that demons are the root cause of the fears, terror, and rage that create emotional stress. Emotional and physical stress weaken the immune system, opening the doorway to illness. Also, I believe that some physical symptoms that feel like "attack," as if an organ or body part has been grabbed or squeezed, may be due to the energetic actions of demons in the subtle energy realm of the body, crossing over into the physical realm.

The New Spirituality

In the new spirituality, people will ascend into higher vibrational frequencies of the 5th and higher dimensions such that there will be no "doorways" for the slower vibrations of negative thoughts, illness, disease, parasitic entities, or possessing demons.

The next chapter presents a method for self-removal of demons, fallen angels, and spirit entities by using a script.

Chapter Eleven

Removal of Spirits and Demons

This chapter offers a script created so people may gain personal relief from attached parasitic spirits and demons. In my experience, however, three other areas require concurrent healing help to provide spiritual wholeness and protection from any type emotional or spiritual attack:

- Healing of the emotional and mental wounds of the inner child, including changed perceptions and integration of the dark side, with forgiveness rather than blame.
- Retrieval of fragmented and lost (or stolen) soul parts that keep a person from being spiritually whole and that provide openings in the energetic bodies in which entities and demons can live.
- Personal empowerment provided by a spiritual reconnection with one's higher self and with God. Feelings of aloneness and separation are replaced with compassion and unconditional love.

Personal Preparation

The preparation that I teach to students who are learning this removal work is summarized in the following list. This is more than is required for using the script, and probably more than most people are willing to put out for their personal well-being:

- The shamanic journey; the shamanic worlds;
- A working relationship with spirit teachers and spirit helpers;
- A working relationship with the archangels Michael, Gabriel, Raphael, and Uriel, the angelic beings, and the Mighty Warriors of Light on Earth;
- An understanding of spirits, demons, fallen angels, the dark forces, the dark beings, and evil;
- A knowledge and acceptance of past wounding of one's inner child, and any resulting lesions that bind fear, shame, or guilt into the physical and energy bodies;
- Some proactive method of healing these inner child wounds (such as hypnotherapy), which leads to forgiveness rather than blaming those seen as the cause of the wounds;
- An understanding and acceptance of one's dark side and personal belief systems (especially beliefs of the devil, demons, and evil);
- An intimate understanding of one's personal fears, their triggering beliefs and emotional responses;
- Ability to use a command voice, issuing from the heart, when exorcizing demons and entities;
- A personal agreement to be impeccable in the use of words and truth with oneself and others, including invisible and non-human beings.

I strongly recommend that unless and until a person has gained some level of personal expertise in each of the above areas, preferably with an experienced teacher, they not attempt these practices with others.

For everyone, I suggest a daily spiritual practice, preferably when it is quiet early in the morning before entering into the events of the day. This should be seen as a time of coming into contact with your inner being and helping powers. Simply close your eyes for the entire time while you call each to join you for the day, remembering to breathe gently and deeply from the belly as you connect. You may find it helpful throughout the connection process to hold the thumb touching your middle and ring finger of each hand. Call on:

- The divine healing light of unconditional love to fill and surround you, providing protection from fear and negativity;
- Your higher self (your spirit) and direct connection with divine guidance and wisdom;
- Your divine self (your upper soul) for truth from your spiritual soul, and for intuitive "ideas" and inspiration for the day ahead;
- Your shadow self (your lower or animal soul) for instinctual truths ("gut instinct") to protect you from harm during the day ahead;
- Your spirit guides, teacher(s) and helper(s) to teach you what you need to know through the day;
- The archangels Michael, Gabriel, Raphael, and Uriel to watch over you and assist you with manifesting desired changes in your life.

The spiritual powers of the archangels and angelic beings are freely available to humans who ask for help (refer to books by psychotherapist Doreen Virtue such as *Healing With The*

Angels: How the Angels Can Assist You in Every Area of Your Life, 1999). The principal archangels I work with are:

- Archangel Michael – "Wayshower" of the light side, God's watcher over Earth and its people, and supreme power over demons and fallen angels;
- Archangel Uriel – power over "clamour and terror" on Earth, and over giant demons;
- Archangel Raphael – master of healing and divine miracles, power over the spirits of humans;
- Archangel Gabriel – master over heaven or paradise and over the portals to the light;
- Mighty Warriors of Light on Earth – special angelic warriors working under command of archangels Michael or Uriel to handle and deliver demons where they need to go so they can be of no harm.

The purpose of a morning connection is to build confidence that your spiritual self and the world of spirit are real, not contrivances of some unknown process of imagination. Trust and faith are born from knowing that you are not alone in who you are and what you are doing, but that you continually are being watched over and loved by God.

Faith is the essential ingredient for personal healing. Because faith is in very short supply in this age and culture, we must nurture and encourage its spread, in contrast to that of skepticism and doubt.

Command Voice

A command voice is not one of regulatory authority or of power over, issuing from the belly and the second chakra, as typically used by military or police officers. Glenda Green, author of *Love Without End: Jesus Speaks* (2000), channeled teachings from Jesus during December 1991, when he "posed" for her, for a portrait as a three-dimensional holographic vision. He taught that "love is the universal instrument of cause and command" and that "love commands the adamantine particles" (p. 66), which he further described as the smallest fundamental and elemental "irreducible" building block of the universe. Everything is built from these particles: storms, bugs, the body, disease. He taught that command is part of our covenant, that "exercising command is central to our dignity. The sole authority for it is love" (p. 67). In summary:

- Our command voice is from the heart, from the position of love, with a firmness of voice that speaks the truth impeccably.
- The resonation of the voice should be felt in the heart and throat to contain a spiritual power that has an impact in the world of spirit.
- It is wise to practice this voice, possibly with children and adults of a rebellious nature, before "commanding" demons; if they rebel you have not yet found the tone and vibration of command.
- In use of command voice, the word "command" is not essential, but may be needed.

Spiritual Authority

As my spirit teacher and the archangel Michael told me, the name of God is given as the spiritual authority for these self-exorcisms. For some, this opens a certain "can of worms" about religion and belief or disbelief in God. I'll attempt to provide some understanding. The use of this name and authority in these scripts is in the "now" and not in the framework or paradigm of thousands of years ago as described in the Old Testament. Now, God is divine source of light and love. The same is true for Jesus. He is, as in a greater sense he has always been, an ascended master teacher, a spiritual being of great wisdom and power, which he is willing to share with others who come to him seeking help. He is universal; he is not a Jew; he is not a Christian. He is divine love and light.

But, to use the scripts, do you need to "believe in" God? Yes, but not in any religious sense. Your personal knowledge of God as the spiritual power and authority for this work is essential to the work. True belief must be part of your command voice.

Some reading this book may feel these practices are forbidden by your religious authorities. I suggest you call on the wisdom of God or Jesus to guide you on your path.

The "Script"

The following script is for personal exorcism. It is for requesting removal of parasitic spirits and demons from yourself, or from your animals, or places that are infested. If someone comes to you in pain, and the presence of parasitic spirits or demons is indicated, the book can be given to them and talked about, and they can use the scripts for themselves, or they can contact a qualified practitioner.

The script for exorcism is not for use with or on others. Reading this book does not make or qualify you as a "depossessor" or exorcist for others. The script is a tool. Use of it does not make you an exorcist any more than having a "power animal" makes you a shaman or having a car makes you a driver. This script can be spoken or read aloud, or silently in your mind.

A Script for Personal Exorcism

I call the archangels Michael and Uriel to help me. I call the Mighty Warriors of Light on Earth to come and surround me.

I ask that a "super bubble" filled with light be placed around any spirit entities, demons, giant demons, shape-shifting giant demons, or fallen angels attached to me.

I call on the archangel Gabriel to open a portal of light and accept any spirits, souls, and soul fragments brought to you.

[With Command Voice] **I command, in the name of God, that all spirit entities, demons, giant demons, shape-shifting giant demons, and fallen angels that are attached to me release their hold on me and step away from me.**

I ask the archangels Michael and Uriel, and the Mighty Warriors of Light on Earth, to remove any spirit entities attached with me and take them to the portal of light; I ask them to remove any demons, shape-shifting giant demons, giant demons, and fallen angels from me and transport them to the "place of confinement" and "womb of transformation."

I call on the divine white healing light of unconditional love, and the archangel Raphael, to come heal the holes and wounds to my physical and energetic body and mind due to any acts and energies of the parasitic beings, including any habits and illnesses that may have formed during that time.

I give thanks of gratitude to the archangels Michael and Uriel and Raphael and Gabriel, and the Mighty Warriors of Light on Earth, for providing help, for carrying out these tasks.

Whether the script "works" as written depends in large part on the faith of you the self-healer, on an absence of fear, at least momentarily, and on emotional intensity in the reading as high or higher than the emotional intensity of the causes of possession. A bland, unemotional reading by an unbelieving reader who is nervous about what he or she is "getting into" may have little result other than attracting more situations that produce fear and disbelief. If that is your situation, I suggest you practice your spiritual connections immediately before reading or saying the script.

The script should be read only once, not several times. If your command voice does not work the first time, there is no reason to think it would a second or third time without more practice or training. Years ago I was working with a dog trainer to teach my young Labrador to heel. When it came my turn to work with the dog, after having watched and heard the trainer, I said, "Heel, heel, heel, *heel.*" The trainer told me, "John, *you* need more training." I thought she had the wrong pronoun, until I noticed her gaze never left my face.

Ritual of Cleansing

Several clients who had had demons attached for many years reported feeling no difference in the days following a depossession or exorcism. In general, following a night's sleep most people experience less noise in the mind, feel renewed energy, feel fewer emotions, and can think more clearly. So, when some indicated that they not only felt no difference but also felt like the parasitic spirits and demons were still present, I knew something was missing.

I asked the advice of my spirit teacher, who told me that a

cleansing ritual was needed for those who had had spirits and/or demons attached for many years, and would be useful for all as a finishing procedure. The reason: around the spirit / human association, there form residual energies, habits, and beliefs that are not removed by removing the parasitic spirits and demons. That certainly resonated with me: I could remember my surprise at times following my own depossession by members of the Brazilian Spiritist Church when, if someone challenged me or my work in some way, I might bristle at them — though not as before, when I was likely to explode into rage. My entire system would be tense and awaiting the explosion. But when, following depossession, the anger or rage didn't come, it took time for me to relax with my new self. Also, the silence in my mind was disquieting; there were no arguments. For perhaps six months I was unsure of who I was, who other people were, and how I was going to react in various situations. There seemed to be more friends in the world. The shedding process was slow. The following ritual will help quicken the process of clearing habits and beliefs incorporated during the time of attached spirits and demons.

This is a ritual around the element of water, which is the natural cleansing element. The elemental power of fire, also a natural cleanser and transformer, is present in the candle. A bathtub or hot tub is appropriate, as is a pool or stream. The ritual is solitary, unless part of a group healing ritual. One candle on or near the tub is adequate, though there is no harm in more. Essential oils may assist the healing process; certainly lavender would be beneficial. The length of time should be enough for the individual to feel cleansed, possibly ten to thirty minutes.

Prior to entering the water, the individual needs to ask to be cleansed of all beliefs and habits, and to state his or her intention of readiness to be cleared. The following is an example:

- I ask to release into the waters all beliefs and habits that I constructed around the parasitic spirits and demons that were in my life.
- I ask the water to receive the energies of these habits and beliefs as they leave me, as a gift from me.
- I ask to have die all images that I hold of myself that derive from parasitic spirits and demons.
- I state my new intention: I am ready to begin life in a new way, a good way, a way that I have not been able to support.
- I am ready to be cleansed of negative energies and hindering habits and beliefs, so that I may be in my life's purpose, so I may be in my sacred contract, so I may be of service to God and the world.
- I ask to be my true self, the pure self that I came into this world to be, cleansed and renewed in power and purpose.

Faith is an essential aspect of ritual. In all cultures, throughout all time, rituals have been used for healing. They have been used because they work. If you should begin having little faith in this process, then you might want to plan on repeating the ritual weekly for several months until you notice a change in your life. You will change. That is certain.

Chapter Twelve

The Dark Beings

In the religious and mythical writings of the past 4,000-plus years, many originating in the "fertile crescent" region ringing the eastern end of the Mediterranean, there is a consistent theme invoking a supernatural dark being who is the leader of demons or forces of the dark, adversary to humankind, and architect of evil in the world. This dark being is invisible, never seen by people, perhaps with the rare exceptions of Buddha and Jesus. Early in their chosen careers, both of those master teachers of spirituality are said to have been tempted by a dark being, to test their strength of character and firmness of resolve.

Several dark beings have been portrayed in Near Eastern and Western literature as the scapegoat of all that is bad, wrong, and evil in the world: Satan or the Devil, Lucifer, Belial, Beelzebub, Mastemah, Ahriman, Semihazah and others. Any one could be the dark being responsible for all the evil on Earth since the beginning. The intent of this chapter is to investigate the origin of the dark beings and determine their relationship with demons and the possession of humans.

Satan – The Devil

The general concept that many of us hold of two dark beings — Satan as the adversary, and the Devil as tempter and tester — or one dark being with two names, originated in versions of the New Testament with which many are familiar. The King James Version, and other versions translated from the Greek, including later Hebrew versions (where devil is written in the Greek, *diabolos*), mention Satan and the Devil as separate beings. Revelation 12:9, a verse containing both names, indicates that both are the same: " ... the dragon, the old serpent, which is the Devil and Satan ..." However, in *The Modern New Testament from Aramaic* (George Lamsa, 1933), translated from original Aramaic text (before the Greek writings), only Satan is present in the text: "...the dragon, that old serpent, which is the Tempter and Satan.... "

Our first meeting with the serpent is in Genesis, where the serpent, the "craftiest" of all the creatures made by God, "tricked" the woman into eating the fruit of the tree of the knowledge of good and evil. For that act, the serpent was cursed by God to crawl on its belly and grovel in dust all the days of its life (Gen. 3:1–15). This could be seen as metaphor, where the Adversary is the serpent, or literally, as a shape-shifting giant demon. The object was the same: tempt the woman with the promise "to be as gods knowing good and evil." That would go against Yahweh's prohibition: "You may freely eat any fruit in the garden, except fruit from the tree of knowledge of good and evil." (Gen. 2:16,17.)

Satan

Further insight into the nature of the Satan of the Old Testament is later found in Job: "One day when the angels came to present themselves before God, Satan, the Accuser, came with them. Where have you come from? the Lord asked Satan. And Satan replied, From Earth, where I've been watching everything that's going on." (Job 1:6,7). Satan, after taunting God, was given God's permission to do what he would with everything that Job had, with the exception of his life (Job 1:12; 2:6). So Satan, the tester, caused Job's sons and daughters, servants, sheep, camels to be slain, and Job to have boils over his entire body. (Job, who at first was "perfect," cursed God and then repented, and ultimately everything was returned to him.) Here, Satan is seen as an angel, a son of God (*ben elohim*), who obeys God's commands. He is equal with the others, but his domain is Earth, not Heaven, though he is not prohibited from Heaven, or chastised on returning.

There is very little of Satan as a proper Hebrew noun (*SaTan*) in the Old Testament. In addition to his presence in Job above, Satan was shown as the cause of King David ordering a census in Israel as the basis of taxation (1 Chron. 21:1). Then in Zechariah, Satan again appeared with high standing in the presence of an angel of the Lord: "Then He showed me Joshua the high priest standing before the angel of the Lord, and Satan standing at his right hand to accuse him." (Zec. 3:1). Otherwise, the common Hebrew noun for adversary, *IsaTan*, is used in several places as when someone is speaking of an enemy (Num. 22:22; 1 Sam. 29:4; 2 Sam. 19:22).

The only contact reported in the Bible between Satan and a human, that with Jesus following his quest of forty days and nights in the desert, is recorded in Mark 1:13, Matthew 4:3–11, and Luke 4:2–13. The King James Version and most other versions of the New Testament translated from early Greek texts, indicate both Satan and the Devil to be present (Matt. 4:10–11). However, again, the translation from original Aramaic, the language of Jesus, has only "the Adversary," SaTan, present as the tempter of Jesus. So Satan and the Devil are synonymous, with one name originating from Aramaic, "Satan," and the other name of Greek origin, "the Devil." Additional dark beings are equated in various literature with Satan.

Ahriman

One of the more detailed views of Satan as the Devil is *The Devil in Legend and Literature* (Maximilian Rudwin, 1973 [original 1931]). He stated that the Devil of Christian religions originated far back in ancient history, in Persia's religion of Zoroastrianism, before 1400 B.C.E., where he had the name Ahriman, or Angra Mainyu, "the evil spirit." Ahriman was the leader of the forces of the dark who were at war with the forces of light led by the god Ahura Mazda. In Zoroaster's view, possibly that of a shaman, as some have suggested, Ahura Mazda made the world as a place where the forces of light could meet in battle with the forces of dark led by Ahriman, so that Ahura Mazda could overcome him and destroy evil.

The Jews learned of these and other religious beliefs, which may have become the basis for their creation stories, the story of the Flood, beliefs in angels and evil, and possibly their legal codes (from Hammurabi), possibly from Abraham (the father of the Jews), who was born near Babylon, or during their captivity in Babylon after the fall of Jerusalem, 587 B.C.E. to about 538 B.C.E., when the first groups returned to Jerusalem (*The Complete Bible Handbook*, John Bowker, 1998).

In my review, there seems to be a marked similarity between Ahriman and Semihazah, leader of the dark forces in the Essenes' *War Scroll*. And my spirit teacher has told me that Zoroaster and the Essenes "had things about right in a metaphoric sense" with their stories.

Semihazah

The writing by Elaine Pagels, *The Origin of Satan* (1995), is to me the most scholarly research regarding Satan's origin and purpose in the world. She recounts that during the Maccabean war (167 B.C.E.) of zealous Jews against ruling Greeks, the *Book of the Watchers* was written, telling how "watcher" angels that God had tasked to watch over Earth, "fell" from heaven. According to Pagels (p. 50), Semihazah was the leader of the watchers who talked 200 other angels into joining him against God's order, as discussed earlier.

From Chapter Nine, we know that in *The Book of Enoch* Satan is linked or equated with Semihazah.

Mastemah-Belial

Pagels (p. 53–54) further indicates that within a few years, another book, called "Jubilees," was written in a similar apocryphal vein, with an underlying message to the people to maintain their ways separate from Gentiles to reduce the conflicts within Jewish communities of the time. The unknown author pointed to the cause of the conflicts: an enemy of the people most often called Mastemah (hatred), Satan, or Belial. The fall of the angels, according to Pagels (p. 54), spawned the giants, who sow violence and evil, and evil spirits, "who are cruel, and created to destroy" (Jub. 10:6). From that time on, the evil spirits are seen to prey on the moral weakness, or ambivalence (the duality, so to speak) of human beings.

The radical Jewish sect called the Essenes, of whom Jesus may have been one, was formed at about the time of the Maccabean war according to Pagels (p. 56). They practiced communal living, "zealousness of the law," and among other devout practices, strict celibacy, possibly because they lived under biblical rules which prohibited sexual intercourse during holy war. The war they saw themselves engaged in, as developed by Pagels, was a war between God and the forces of evil, with the Essenes in the center of that cosmic war. One of their sacred books found with other scrolls in the caves at Qumran was the *War Scroll* (1QM; 4Q491–496).

The Authors of the *Dead Sea Scrolls* (Wise, Abegg, Jr., and Cook, 1996) indicate that the *War Scroll* described seven battles between the forces of light and dark. One ally of Belial and enemy of the light was called "the Kittim," taken by the authors to be a coded name for the Roman occupation rulers of Israel (since 63 B.C.E.). In the seventh and final battle, "the great hand of God shall overcome [Belial and all] the angels of his dominion, and all the men of [his forces shall be destroyed forever]" (1QM 1: 14-15). Belial and his followers were described further:

And cursed is Belial for his contentious purpose ... and cursed are all the spirits of his lot for their wicked purpose. Accursed are they for all their filthy dirty service. For they are the lot of darkness, but the lot of God is light [eternal] (1QM 13:4–6).

[To God] You appointed the Prince of Light from of old to assist us, for in [His] l[ot are all sons of righteous]ness and all spirits of truth are in his dominion. You yourself made Belial for the pit, and angel of malevolence, his [dominio]n is in darkne[ss] and his counsel is to condemn and convict. All the spirits of his lot — the angels of destruction — walk in accord with the rule of darkness, for it is their only [des]ire. (1QM13: 10–12).

Pagels (p. 58) quotes the same passage from the *War Scrolls* from a different translation, which says that Satan (as Belial) is the angel Mastemah. Thus it appears that Mastemah, Belial, and Satan are different names for the same being, indicating the different natures of a supernatural being who led the forces of darkness in battle, whether metaphoric or literal, against the forces of light. Semihazah, as a leader of "fallen angels," may be equivalent to Mastemah, as is Ahriman.

Satan, as Rival Religions

From his Christian Brothers' Catholic background, Peter Stanford (*The Devil: A Biography*, 1996), with extensive historical review, concludes, "Few educated people today believe in the Devil as a reality" (p. 13). Yet he shows that religions have portrayed and continue to portray the Devil as aligned with any "evil" rival religious teachings. The Jews did this with the Greeks and Romans, the early Christians with the Gnostics, the Roman Catholics with any practices of pagan animism or shamanism, Martin Luther and the Protestants with the Catholics, and the Christians with the Jews and Muslims, etc.

This practice led to religious hatred, crusades, and wars killing millions of people. And various groups of people were targeted for extermination through the ages as a result of these religious teachings: witches, healers, Cathars, Freemasons, seductive women, Gypsies, Jews, sorcerers, magicians, and shamans.

Journey to Satan

One way for me to obtain answers, whether metaphoric or literal, to resolve who Satan is and whether he is leader of the demons, would be to journey to the source. Prior to this journey, I asked of my pendulum, "Is there a Devil? Is there a Satan?" I got negatives to both. Still, I had some trepidation as I heard my ego recount a quick list of "what ifs" about the possibility of not returning. I asked for silence from my know-it-all inner voice, and felt determined to go looking for answers. With my same team for spiritual guidance and protection as in earlier journeys, I dove into the lower levels of the Middle World. As we were going downward, with the driving rapid drumbeat, Eagle was telling me, "There is no one of that name." Not assured, I asked her to stop at each level so I could call to find out; nothing occurred on the first or second levels.

On the third level, as I called out to the Devil, a black-suited, horned and tailed person appeared saying he was the Devil. We all looked closely, and he looked real, but then his edges began shifting slightly, then wavering, as if he were not quite solid. I asked who he was and he replied, "I'm the true leader of the dark forces. The one you saw in the cavern making demons is my stand-in when I'm busy." Bear handed me a bucket of water, which I threw on the Devil as we all stood watching. He screamed curses and began smoking and sizzling and dissolving as he slowly oozed into the floor until he was a puddle. Cougar walked over and drank the entire puddle.

We walked to deeper levels as I called out for Satan. Finally, a man dressed in a black robe with a tall stand-up collar appeared, striding fiercely toward us. I felt again as I did at the first sudden appearances of Darth Vader in *Star Wars*. My breath caught for a moment, and I tensed as I waited for the rasping, breathy voice. But the voice was clear, deeply pitched, and filled with warning as he asked, "What do you want?" Feeling adventurous (and wanting to check out his suggestibility), I walked up and bumped into him, saying contact with me would burn him badly, at which he jumped back. I did it again, and he cursed as he burnt his hand fending me off. Then I turned a flashlight, provided by Bear, on him. The light burned holes through him until he was no more.

I asked my spirit teacher (merged within me) what the "Devil" and "Satan" were, and he replied, "Apparitions. They have no life force of their own, only the breath of life blown into them that is the thought of their creator. You were their creator, and the power of your imagination and your expectation of what you feared you would see was what created them. Your beliefs came from the myths and fictions created by early Christian leaders who maintained positions of power, held on to existing church members, and brought in new followers by creating a haven of safety from evil and fear. The amount of energy that you project into the apparitions is the amount they can use to hurt you. They have power, and can cause harm equal to your imagination, beliefs, and fears. But that's because people allow their fears and imaginations to be engaged and manipulated by happenings of their past, including what you would call past lives, that have had fearful and unresolved outcomes, and have had fearful and false religious teachings. Then those people are open to suggestions, by possessing demons and "demonic" spirit entities, to create these devil apparitions to play out the challenging emotions of their dark side that they still haven't resolved."

He continued with the teaching: "People believe the apparent thoughts of these devilish apparitions because they align with their core beliefs. The apparitions can't think; they just mirror and feed back people's core beliefs to them. Many people believe that they should fear any being of a certain appearance, often described as "terrifying," which creates a self-fulfilling prophecy. As the fear and terror in the people escalate, the apparition continues to mirror, intensify, and feed back the fearful and terrifying thoughts into their runaway imaginations. If someone feels worthless in his core, and a very strong persona comes to him agreeing he's worthless, he may jump off a bridge to get rid of the feeling and the voice in his head. Or he may follow the directive of a voice that promises to make him rich and famous. There you have the makings for a movie like *The Devil's Advocate*, the story of a young, vain, successful attorney and his attractive, greedy wife, both ripe for the picking by the elder who promises them anything. He can promise them anything because he has sold his soul to the temptations of the Devil for his power over and riches and illusions, and he lies about everything, without concern for his soul's evolution. What the couple gets is a strong reality of torment and destruction, their 'hell on Earth.'"

The journey came to a stop as I attempted to revise many years of mythical belief in my mind.

Summary

In summary, Satan is not a real being or real spirit being. On the other hand, Satan *is* real due to the many millions of people who have believed in Satan over thousands of years. Satan is as real as beliefs are real. Satan can and does exist in people's minds as a religious belief, a moral concept, an apparition, an archetype, or as a spiritual presence. Those who have been subjected to ritual satanic abuse have the name of Satan burned in their minds and souls as a real being. Satan can exist as a personal demon, an internal adversary composed by the ego in opposition to the true self, as he may have appeared to Jesus in the desert wilderness. Or, Satan, Mastemah, Belial, Azazel (and other names reviewed above) may be names used by Jewish and later Christian writers to hide the identity of a spirit being who is the "true" leader of demons and evil spirits. Or, that identity might have been unknown to those writers.

Lucifer

Rudwin (*The Devil in Legend and Literature,* 1973 [original 1931]) opens his extensive review of literature of the Devil with the following (p. 1):

> The legend of Lucifer has no biblical basis. The ancient Hebrews knew of no devil whatever. Satan in the Old Testament is no devil in the accepted meaning of the word. He was originally not an adversary but an adjutant of the Almighty. Satan was a member of the celestial court and stood high in the councils of Jehovah. He belonged to the assembly of the sons of God, but sat on the opposition bench.

Rudwin further writes, "The substitution of Lucifer for Satan as the rebel angel is a contribution by the Christian fathers. It is a result of a wrongly interpreted biblical passage" (p. 3)

Journey to Lucifer

I continued my interrupted journey: we went deeper, and into the Lower World, to find and meet with Lucifer for more answers. I wondered at a historical being with the name of "light-giver" or "bearer of light" or "morning star" being portrayed by many other writers, especially religious ones, as the leader of evil forces on the basis of a long-standing misinterpretation.

In the Bible, Isaiah questions: "How are you fallen from heaven, O shining star, son of the morning! You have been thrown down to the earth, you who destroyed the nations of the world." (Is. 14:12). The King James Version alone translates "day star" into Lucifer, which is a Latin name, not Hebrew, meaning "light-bearer" (Pagels, *The Origin of Satan,*1996). Prior to about 1980, this was taken to portray the casting out of heaven of the archangel Lucifer. But, according to the *Illustrated Dictionary and Concordance of the Bible* (1986), the writing in Isaiah referred to the death of a king of Babylon, who died about 750 B.C.E. at the time the verse was written.

The legend of Lucifer, created by Jewish and Christian writers long after the Bible was written (for example, John Milton's *Paradise Lost* (1667–1674), is that he was highest in the heavenly hierarchy of angels, greatest in power, wisdom, beauty, and love of God, with dominion over the Earth. But, due to jealousy of the other seven archangels, or as usually supposed by most writers, due to personal pride and ambition in opposition to God, Lucifer was banished from Heaven into the dark depths of Earth.

Many writers, including Baldwin (*Spirit Releasement Treatment,* 1995), have said that Lucifer — possibly an archangel of the earliest times — having been thrown out of "heaven" to Earth by the archangel Michael, is the leader and "consciousness" of the dark forces.

Continuing downward in my journey, myriad thoughts of Lucifer flooding my consciousness, my spirit helpers brought me to a huge, high-ceilinged room gleaming with the blackness of obsidian. There, I saw Lucifer as a beautiful, awesome being radiating a glistening black, and though mostly hidden, there were the obvious shapes of wings above his high shoulders. He greeted our arrival and I told him we had looked for the Devil and Satan and had found only apparitions. He laughed and said, "That's all there have ever been. But that does not keep people from fantasizing them into solid reality in your world and then having more trouble on their hands than opening a hornet's nest in the house. Because once created, they are real and must be dealt with. They become a life challenge to overcome. Had you called out different names at different places and levels of the world, you would have created and seen different fearful apparitions. Or, if you went in a totally non-fearful frame of mind, not thinking fearful thoughts, not visualizing fearful fantasies, you could have found apparitions of grace and beauty to match your search. What you create them with is what maintains them, what feeds them. Fear maintains fearful creations; love maintains loving creations; passivity and apathy maintain nothing, so without attention, without feeding, your creations die."

I asked if he would be willing to explain his role in the world. He was gracious and clear in his agreement. "I watch over the dark side of humanity. I am the Wayshower for the evolution of the dark side of the human self, according to the divine plan of the Creator God, as my brother Michael does over the light side. I have no control or say over the demons of the dark forces. *You* can teach them, enlighten them into their true purpose or mission, which is to combine their light and power with that of angelic beings. This merger will create a special angelic being and will produce ... [some great power of healing that I couldn't understand]. Reach out to the dark forces to begin a dialog. Move into a teaching of the dark side."

I was taken aback by the personal nature of his remarks. Not knowing what to say, and avoiding his suggestions, I asked for further explanation of his purpose. He continued, "I maintain the darker polarity of your earthly duality so your physical and spiritual consciousness may have the greatest potential for limitless expansion of the self, the God-self, and God. You on Earth call the darker polarity "bad" or "evil." I do not cause evil, nor do I create evil. In your reality, all that goes on in your world called evil has been created by humans, not by me, and not by or of God. I provide the adverse of light in all situations of spiritual choice, which is why I have been know as the adversary since the oldest times. As many of these situations appear to be temptations to the greedy human appetites for accumulation, including money, power over others, war to gain territory and resources, sensory stimulation and control through sex, and experiencing and causing intense sensations such as pain and terror, I am known as tempter and devil. But all these appetites and desires are of human choice, development, and endeavor. They are manifested into physical reality through the sequence of intent and belief, or thought, or dream. None of these have I created. Without the dark polarity, there would be no incentive for human movement and evolution through the expansion of consciousness. But the evolution over time from dark to light, unconscious to conscious, duality to unity, asleep to awake as regards soul's life purpose, God-in-heaven to God-in-self, has been a human movement, an expression of free will."

I remarked that I found it "coincidental" that his home was "beneath," in some cosmological sense, the cavern of the demons, and asked if there was some linkage between him and the demons of the dark forces. He smiled and said, "I see you are working at unraveling an ancient secret of Lucifer and the dark forces. When you read the newspaper, you may notice a certain number of horrible events each day in each country of the world. They provide headlines and television images that cause people to gasp in horror. But that also keeps them from having to go out and do those things themselves to see and feel how they turn out. In other words, many, many people do not have to explore their darkest dark sides because they can see it acted out in their paper each morning and on TV every night. Of course, no one needs to watch every night, to get his dark-side needs met vicariously. But, some fear that if they don't get their nightly fix, they might become the next raving serial killer. The same thing is provided the teenagers by the horror movies."

I thanked him for this darkly illuminating information, and we returned to the Middle World the way we had come. Lucifer appears to have some power to regulate the numbers of "horrific" incidents that happen on Earth, as if he is a kind of master guardian angel, despite his saying he has no control. There may be no overt control, but somewhere there is an energetic regulator that adjusts dark actions to provide a strange balance and harmony to the world of dark and light. Lucifer has not "fallen" in any sense except in his reputation among humanity. With respect to pride, he appeared amazingly humble.

Summary of Lucifer

I understood Lucifer's statement that he is a brother to the archangel Michael to mean that he too is an archangel, meaning he is a messenger of God for us on Earth. He is with us on Earth as a spiritual being to help us develop our personal dark sides by providing testing situations. It is our choice whether we develop the power of our dark sides in the way of creativity or of evil. Religions have given Lucifer the reputation of Satan, and have used him as a scapegoat onto which to project all that they and their adherents declare is evil in the world. From this we have wars, genocide, inquisitions, and many forms of witch-hunt. We learn to use Lucifer as a whipping boy for each of us to project our own evil upon. Then we remain ignorant and in denial of tendencies and archetypes we carry in our personal dark sides. We do not have to own or be responsible for our internal terrorist that keeps us fearful of terrifying urges, the internal torturer that keeps us in pain over past wounds, the internal rapist that violates our trust of our self, the internal murderer that kills our creative urges, the internal prostitute that sells out for money or power over, and the internal saboteur that pulls the rug from under us just as we are about to come into our true purpose and self. Only world-shaking events like September 11, 2001 have the shock of a cosmic two-by-four hitting us "upside the head" to awaken us to the consciousness of our true inner nature.

When we refuse to take advantage of great events to awaken spiritually and personally to the unknown riches of our true self and our true life purpose, we are in essence demanding that Creator arrange some massive personal event, such as losing a job, divorce, disability, cancer, stroke, heart attack, or AIDS, to open us to our truth. And, as with dreams prophesying our future, if we don't make notes and put into effect changes in our lives, the consciousness raised by life-shaking events will not be well utilized. Creator patiently will begin searching for a larger teaching to answer our requests to awaken.

Beelzebub

Beelzebub is said to have been an ancient god of the Babylonians or Phoenicians, called "lord of the flies" or "fly-god," which forms a link to the Persian leader of the dark forces, Ahriman. Beelzebub is said by Rudwin (p. 3, 21) to have entered the world as a fly. In various translations of the Bible he is called Beelzebul,

Beelzeboul (Hebrew), Beelzavow (Aramaic), Baalzebub, Baalzebul. Baal was the name of a community in Northern Syria; also the name of a fertility god of the Canaanite people (*The New Smith's Bible Dictionary*, W. Smith, 1966).

Earlier, when I was pursuing an understanding of the role of Satan, I asked my spirit teacher for an explanation of Satan as described in Job 1:6, 7, and received the following: "The being that is described as the Adversary of God is one whose name is not speakable or knowable by humans. The nearest that it has come to being said is 'Beelzebub.' This was a name used in public by the Pharisees when attempting to trap Jesus into confessing that he used the authority of the leader of demons for his exorcisms. It was a grandiose attempt to illustrate their esoteric wisdom over Jesus' in matters of demons and exorcism. Therefore, Satan and Beelzebub are in a sense the same names for the same being, except that Satan describes only one of the many natures of Beelzebub, that of Adversary."

The Pharisees, high priests of the temple of Jerusalem at the time of Jesus, called Beelzebub the "head of the demons." The earlier biblical introduction of the name is through Ahaziah, the eighth king of Israel and king of Samaria (904–892 B.C.E.), who suffered sickness from a fall. He sent messengers, telling them, "Go, inquire of Baal-zebub, the god of Ekron, whether I shall recover from this sickness" (2K 1:2). At the time, Baal-zebub was seen as only slightly less powerful in certain areas than El, the Hebrew God usually called Jehovah, and there were altars in Israel to him (Smith, *The New Smith's Bible Dictionary*, 1966).

Trying to show an alignment of Jesus with this dark being, The Pharisees reportedly accused Jesus in public of using the authority of Beelzebub to cast out demons. But Jesus countered,

"If I use Satan to cast out Satan, he is divided against himself. So if I cast out demons by Beelzebub, by what do your own people cast them out? ... And if I cast out demons by the spirit of God, then the kingdom of God has come near you." (Matt. 12:24–28, Mark 3:22–26).

Jesus' question to the Pharisees illustrates his understanding that the exorcism of demons and unclean spirits requires the authority of a higher order of spirit being than the demons — either Beelzebub, apparently the most powerful dark being, or God, acknowledged as the most powerful being of light. If the Pharisees answer that their exorcists also use the name of Beelzebub, the leader of demons, then they are guilty of the same "crime" of which they are accusing Jesus.

Who or what was this Beelzebub? My spirit teacher told me that the Essene writings about Mastemah as a "Prince of Darkness" and leader of the forces of darkness are similar to the nature of Beelzebub, but that Beelzebub did not "fall" from Heaven, and that there is more to Beelzebub that is unknowable, including his true name.

Beelzebub is not much in the public consciousness, and has not been for the past 2,000 years. Modern authors include discussion of the name because it occurs in the New Testament, where Jesus is accused of using the leader of the demons as his authority for casting out demons (Matt. 12:24–28, Mark 3:22–26), not because they have anything new to add to this brief knowledge.

Shamanic Journey To Beelzebub

Again, I decided that a shamanic journey would be the only way to find this apparent supreme leader of the dark forces, and the only means of obtaining personalized information, whether literal or metaphoric. Asking to be taken to the place of Beelzebub, I set out with my "team," intending to learn his purpose and his relationship to other dark beings. After traveling quite some time through dark night and swirling winds, I came to a high, jet-black mountain. Around the peak lightning flashed and thunder crashed. I went to a door near the top of the mountain, where I asked to see Beelzebub. I was laughed at by several gatekeepers, who said I had the wrong name. I said I knew the true name, but that I would not speak it. A lengthy discussion followed, in which I was given various warnings and threatened with death if I were lying about the name. Finally, I was admitted and taken to Beelzebub.

The whole place was dark, with light reflected only from various furnaces and fires operating at scattered locations, as in an old-fashioned ironworks. A giant man, much taller than I, with dark, scowling features, approached me. He agreed, in a very deep, strong voice, that I could call him Beelzebub and that he would speak with me. I asked his purpose in the world. He answered, "I am part of the beginning; without darkness there could be no light. I was created to maintain a world where humans could have the experience of free will, could come to understand the duality, light and dark, good and evil, above and below, within and without. My purpose on Earth is to maintain the integrity of the separation between the dark and the light, to maintain the boundary of the darkness. The dark has a force, a power to create, that is weakened if the boundary becomes breached or porous."

He paused to look at me in a questioning but threatening way. I said nothing, so he continued: "The Dark Force holds the universe in position in ways that are not understood. I also create separation in humans, so they feel as individuals, alone. I also test human free will, creating trials and challenges by providing situations for the processes of abandonment, betrayal, emotional abuse, physical abuse, sexual abuse, stealing power from a child, and creating traumatic incidents that weaken self-esteem in growing children. The more challenge a person has requested for a lifetime in his life contract, the more severe and ongoing is the challenge. My purpose is to continually test people, to weaken their character and strength of purpose, and tempt them to the dark forces."

I asked Beelzebub whether he is an angel. He replied, "You could call me an archangel, as I was created in the beginning along with the other seven to make a full octave. Yet, from the beginning, by choice, my domain and responsibility has been Earth, not Heaven." (The other archangels named in the Bible are Michael, Gabriel, and Raphael. In addition, the Ethiopian book of *Enoch* lists Uriel, Raguel, Zerachiel, and Remiel. Metatron, "with seventy-two mystical names," is mentioned in Jewish lore as the prince of all angels, and could be in a different rank from the archangels [Connolly, *In Search of Angels*, 1994]).

At this point in the journey I began to feel very sleepy, desiring to slip away from consciousness. I had an image of Dorothy in the *Wizard of Oz,* caught sleeping in the field of poppies and carried away by demons to the castle of the wicked witch. The thought of where that might end shocked me awake.

I asked Beelzebub about his relationship to Lucifer. He told me, "Near the beginning, I asked the Creator God for an intermediary, a messenger. So Lucifer was sent. He is a twin, what you might call a clone, of the archangel Michael, and thus is also an archangel. His task on Earth is to work with the consciousness of the dark side of human divinity. Within the dark side, or the shadow self, is all of the creativity and passion for life of the true self. This also is the "wild self," which contains all the ability of the human for survival, personal defense and protection, freedom and wildness, and more. Lucifer brings directions from above to this place. We work together to create the optimum conditions for the experiments of the Creator to work. At times he has created Satan to appear to those on Earth who call out, demanding that he appear. He uses the same process that I use to create my helping angels. I like that he has been recognized as the source of evil; in that way I remain behind the scenes and out of human consciousness."

Beelzebub remains out of consciousness by allowing other names to be credited with his activities. But all of them might be him, so I asked about his relationship with Satan. He said, "Through the identity of Satan, I appear as the adversary of God. I appear as the helping power of those who have gone over to the dark forces through their greed and seduction by power over, and causing pain in, others. Satan, that aspect of me, keeps the separation of good and evil distinct. He maintains duality with sharp boundaries, so the one does not begin to blend with the other and lose its identity. But duality is not about opposites; it is about forces that are totally different. And notice how well he has done: people still react to evil with the same shock as they did 5,000 and 10,000 years ago, and longer. Everyone needs an adversary. And the stronger the person desires to be, the stronger the adversary must be in order that the resolve can be fully tested. Strength of character is built through testing and adversity, not through eating ice cream."

That felt like a personal shot, not that I was eating ice cream at the moment. But then, he directed my attention to a person-sized crystal ball that was being rolled from its final furnace to a cooling rack. He asked if I would like to see my future.

I responded, skeptically, that I would look over his shoulder while he checked it out. Nevertheless, a view of me sitting in an elaborate chair with crimson and gold robes, as if a king on a throne, materialized within the ball. People were around me, sitting and standing, as if listening to everything I had to say, but looking somewhat listless. I told him I wasn't interested in that kind of future; that my purpose is increasing my consciousness and empowering others through healing and teachings, not taking away their power by holding them captive as students and followers. A fleeting sneer crossed his face as I spoke. I felt a strong urge in my body to change my opinion, but was determined to hold my ground.

I asked whether he was the creator of the lesser demons. With a self-congratulatory smirk he said, "You humans generate all these 'renewable and sustainable' resources, emotions and negative thoughts, and leave them lying around on the Earth's surface. So, being adverse to waste, from early times I began collecting and running these through a mold where they could be compressed thousands of times and given a spark of life. Then, I ask them to help me with my mission, warn them not to fail, and turn them loose on the Earth to torment humans, create chaos in their lives, intensify fears, create separation from God and tribe, and drive people to the dark forces."

I became aware of being on the verge of falling asleep again. Also, I was feeling overwhelmed by this dark force I was standing with, and had a sense of power draining from me. Subtle processes were happening, draining my energy, my self-esteem, and my personal power. It was time to leave, in a hurry. So with brief good-byes I left this dark being, the leader of the dark forces, leader of the manufactured demons, and returned to the starting point of my journey.

Summary

Beelzebub is the force and power of darkness, the "true" leader of the dark forces, the creator of demons, the spiritual being that, appearing as an adversary of God and humans has been called Satan or the Devil and other similar names. He is the being that has been responsible for acts of darkness blamed on Lucifer, and the being who has been here since the beginning. He works with the demons and dark forces to keep humans from remembering their oneness with God and their spiritual purpose on Earth. His intent is to create the dark illusion of separation that has driven some to deep despair and the "dark night of the soul." He creates the illusion that the "endpoint" of an experimental material world of free will, negativity, and duality, this planet Earth, is aloneness with fear and evil, rather than togetherness in unity and love.

The New Spirituality

There is no spiritual intent to create pain, or terror, or evil. They have been created from the beliefs of humanity. In the new spirituality we will be conscious that to learn and practice compassion and unconditional love does not require a Satan. An adversary and fear will no longer be needed as primary teachers. The state of being of Creator is "I am love," and that is All That Is.

Chapter Thirteen is about the dark forces. I have used the words "dark forces" previously without explanation. The intent of the next chapter is to explore the concept and reality of dark forces as they pertain to possession, demons, and the nature of evil in the world.

Chapter Thirteen

The Dark Forces (and Evil)

Ancient Dark Forces

The intent of the dark forces has remained the same through time: destroy the forces of light through evil actions. The dark forces have been described by various ancient writers: by Zoroaster sometime between 2000 and 1400 B.C.E., by an unknown Jewish Maccabean author less than 200 years before Jesus, and by an unknown Jewish Essene at about the same time or somewhat later than the previous.

Seemingly, over time, people would have been protected against evil by laws. The earliest written laws and codes of a legal system to correct "injustice" originated in Sumeria (present-day Iraq) about 2600 B.C.E. And that was a "reform" decree some 700 years before the code of Hammurabi, the Babylonian king often credited with the first code of law (Sitchin, *The 12th Planet: Book I of the Earth Chronicles*, 1978). The first Sumerian civilization, according to ancient texts, was Eridu, found near the Persian Gulf, the foundation of which has been dated at 3800 B.C.E. (Sitchin, p. 49). This predates by some 500 to 1,000 years the cultures of Egypt, Indus Valley, China, and the Celts of Europe.

Sitchin indicates that the king of Eridu wrote that his god had told him "to restore the decree of former days," indicating there was an older code. The "evils" to be righted by the reforms were listed as: "primarily the unfair use by the supervisors of their powers to take the best for themselves; the abuse of official status; the extortion of high prices by monopolistic groups" (p. 43). The same injustices are with us today.

The laws of the Hebrews, the Ten Commandments, were said in the Old Testament to have been given to Moses on Mt. Sinai about 1500 B.C.E. (Ex. 31:18; 34:28) some 400 years after the Babylonian laws. The presence of laws does not prove, but presents *prima facie* evidence of wrongdoing in those earliest times. The proliferation of codes, laws, and rules and regulations in every culture since indicates that wrongdoing has continued, and that laws in themselves are ineffective at prohibiting evil actions and the dark forces. The more extreme injustices have been called "evildoing," usually shortened to "evil." This has led to people, rather than their actions, being judged as evil.

With the advent of Christianity, in its variations, the dark forces, over much of the next 2,000 years, became who or whatever was the designated enemy of the religion pointing its finger. The Inquisition, Crusades, and conquests of native populations in France, England, South America, Mexico, North America, Australia, and Africa occurred in the name of cross and crown of various empires. The "bad guys" were hard to identify, since many appeared to wear white hats. Only with some spiritual clarity, perceptive insight, and factual information could the truth be seen.

Modern Dark Forces

Saraydarian *(Battling the Dark Forces,* 1998, p. 14) indicated the "dark forces are those who work for evil purposes behind the veil, subjectively and in secret." He said they damage and destroy only the parts of humans that are susceptible to being corrupted, the parts that have the predisposition to hatred, revenge, separatism, drugs, alcohol, prostitution, and the black arts. People who are caught in the web of the dark forces oppose or hate beauty, goodness, righteousness, joy, freedom, enlightenment, expansion of consciousness, clarity of thought, and contact with the inner self. They hate others who are light and joyful, living in spiritual peace and harmony, and will attempt to pull them down into the gloom and darkness where they live through attacking vulnerable beliefs, weaknesses of self-esteem, and areas of ignorance.

In my work, I have come to realize that demons, as described in Chapter Nine, are agents of the dark forces. All around us, they watch and wait for us to open a doorway, an opening or hole into the subtle energy body of the human, into which they can enter.

Some of my clients would like to blame the possessing entity or demon for their actions, but the entity or demon is not to blame for the possession. Only the person who becomes possessed makes the conscious or subconscious choice to open his or her particular doorway to the demon. All of the following have been used as excuses: "My wounded inner child made me vulnerable." "I don't know how this happens." "They did it to me before I could set up my protection." "If you hadn't told me about demons, I wouldn't be bothered by them." "I'm worse now (repressed emotions emerging) than before the healing."

"You didn't say that could happen!" Excuses are based on a belief that others are responsible for one's life, and to blame for feeling victimized. Excuses are irrelevant, and they only obscure awareness of the possession process.

The dark forces appear to operate on many planes and in many forms. Sarydarian (p. 219–227) said that their control operates from the astral plane, but that the dark forces occur on all lower planes and include human beings who have lost or sold their souls to the dark forces. Also, he said that they include non-human entities from the astral plane. Therefore, the dark forces are operational in both the spiritual and the physical, human and non-human realms.

That there are humans involved in dark acts with horrible outcomes is obvious, and undeniable to citizens of this country since September 11, 2001. There are three kinds of humans who may get snared in the web of the dark forces:

1. People intrigued or obsessed by their dark sides, their shadow self, who give in to urges to commit horrible acts;

2. People possessed by demonic-type spirit entities and demons who are driven to commit acts of a horrific nature; and

3. People possessed by multiple demonic-type spirit entities and demons, or demons driven sufficiently by desire for power over others, and who may find enough pleasure (or relief) in the horrific acts imagined by their dark sides to trade or sell their souls to the dark forces. Some of these people probably incarnate in multiple lives, where the same demon awaits their "coming" to repossess them and take them deeper into experiencing the urges and imaginings of their dark sides, and their associations with the dark forces.

From readings I have done, the last typifies the serial killer-rapist-torturer and terrorist (who is all the others in one package). These are probably individuals, operating alone and in secret, perhaps known only to their victims and the police. Others, however, may be leaders, in which case they probably have others of their kind in their service. The leaders most likely have sold their souls for promises of money or some type of power over people. Throughout history, those aligned with the dark forces at the top of the leadership pyramid have traded their souls for leadership of large organizations, religions, or countries. The usual contractual statement would be very simple, accompanied by vehement emotion: "I'd give anything to be able to run this [specify name of the country, corporation, or religion]!" And, as this has the intent of a prayer to spirit, if this issue is written in the person's life contract, the true essence of the request is immediately granted, or at least the wheels of synchronicity are started in motion at a pace appropriate to the true intent of the statement.

Healing the Dark Side

How can we be finished with the secret darkness of our dark sides so we are not so vulnerable to judgmental feelings of guilt and shame that we could be in the power of another? The healing requires each person to acknowledge his or her dark side. When you read or hear any story of drunkenness, violence, murder, rape, or torture that hooks you into feeling angry or vengeful, sad or sympathetic, acknowledge how those feelings relate to your dark side. In other words, if you have beaten someone and feel guilty of the act, denying that a story of someone beating another to death pertains to you is lying to yourself. To provide healing, call the divine white healing light of unconditional love down through the crown of your head, to thoroughly fill your body, and then visualize the light going deep into the Earth as an anchor.

Acknowledge the repressed aspects of your dark side as "characters" or sub-personalities of your self. Allow them one at a time to come into your consciousness. First, you must accept each as "you." Then you must re-label the judgment you originally formed about this piece of "you," not by changing "bad" to "good," which is being stuck in the third-dimensional illusion of "duality." Instead, consistent with the energy of the new millennium, select a revised label in view of the true needs of humans. For example, you may have committed an act that you believed to be violent and judged as "bad." On reevaluation, you may see that you were attempting to express your need for love without knowing how, and became angry at rejection. Re-labeling will permit you to see your self in new light. Compassion, empathizing rather than feeling sorry for, and forgiveness of self, without judgment, are the next steps. Then this former "character" of your dark side can be accepted and integrated with the "others" of your conscious (light) self.

Evil

Throughout recorded history, the word "evil" has been used to create in the minds of listeners and readers everything that can be imagined as the polar opposite of "good":

- of sinister intention;
- graphically horrible and ugly;
- unrelentingly cruel;
- ever-increasingly painful without end;

- overpowering, such that our physical strength is puny;
- without moral conscience to be appealed to;
- with the strewing of imaginary blood and guts to all quarters of the landscape of the mind.

The word "evil" calls to mind elements of the supernatural, with graphic images of gargoyles, demons, devils, and part-human beasts conjured up by the single word. Religions connect the word with actions purportedly performed by Satan, the Devil, or by humans whose actions are directed Satan.

This word has been used to explain millions of horrific acts. The imprint of the word is even more powerful since the advent of newspapers, magazines, and television, where the word — four brief keystrokes — can define true-life events by showing real blood, real guts, real tears, and real feelings of terror spread over a real landscape.

Virtually no other word has this visceral impact. Some that come close are hate, terror, terrorist, rage, enemy, death, hell, alone, rape, incest, famine, gruesome, bound, and powerless. For a few, in certain context, "the other" has chilling connotations. Every writer and public speaker has favorites with which to paint indescribable word pictures for his or her audience. I have, therefore, come to the conclusion that those who use the word to describe some horrific action of inhumanity have a conscious or subconscious intention to create fear in their listening and reading audiences.

I am amazed at the speeches made by two presidents of the United States, which should be the most educated country in the world, stating that there is an "evil axis" (George Bush) or "evil empire" (Ronald Regan). This is so naively simplistic as to make one question the knowledge of the speechwriters. In spite of the fact that ancient Persia and Babylon (present-day Iran and Iraq) are ancient birthplaces of demonology and angelology, there are no evil empires and no evil axis. Throughout history there have been countries controlled by leaders who have sold their souls, gone over to the dark forces, and perpetuate evil actions among their people, but the countries are not evil, and the religions of the people are not evil.

Everything indicates that there are people with evil intent on Earth, and those people commit actions that are evil; they cause terrorism, wars, and great crimes against individuals and communities. Some would say that these humans have been corrupted by the dark forces and the forces of evil. It is truer to say that they have been tempted and tested by the demons, and that they have accepted whatever temptation was offered in trade for their souls. Then, they moved from the realm of terrible actions to evil actions, in alignment with the dark forces.

From Lucifer

In my earlier journey to Lucifer in the Lower World, I asked him about evil. He told me: "Evil is the darkest of a person's dark side abilities put into being with the intent to create pain and gain power-over through tyranny. Evil is performed in support of dark forces both in physical and spiritual forms. There is a leader and organization to the dark forces."

While true that each of us has a dark side, thankfully it is also true that not all of us intend to create pain and gain power over others through oppressive action.

From Beelzebub

During my journey to Beelzebub, described in the previous chapter, I challenged him as creator of all that is evil in the world. He laughed and indicated that he felt it funny that humans gave him so much power. In calling him "evil," or calling "evil" certain actions attributed to someone or something like him, people create fear about the possibility of evil within their own dark sides, thereby giving up some of their own power. In his creation and use of the lesser demons as a force of darkness, Beelzebub said, he intended only to offer people a complete understanding of this physical world, with full options for humans in any lifetime to experiment with a full range of actions and outcomes.

"For hundreds of thousands of years," he told me, "people have been pointing their fingers at me and crying 'evil' for various actions and events, but I am not here to cause pain and suffering. There is no intent in me, or within Creator God, to cause pain and suffering. It was humans who developed the use of pain and suffering to reinforce the learning of lessons in the physical reality of Earth. Calling certain actions and the people responsible for them 'evil' was also a human act. But there were other beings involved, who came here from realms outside yours, who had greater power and technology than yours, and some of them gained pleasure from actions that caused people pain and suffering. Invariably, those acts were termed 'evil' by others, particularly those who gain favor by giving speeches about the evil of others to keep the spotlight of truth from their own heads."

I didn't particularly want to disturb the flow of information from this being who seemed to know the origin of many things considered mysteries on Earth. He continued, "But, back to Earth's people. Throughout time there have been individuals who have written in their life contracts an intention to investigate their dark sides in depth — beings like Adolf Hitler and Joseph Stalin, who, as national leaders, killed millions, great pain and suffering marking the deaths. That lifetime was neither their first nor will it be their last of bringing periods of twin horrors to the world. But in its history, every country has had leaders who have caused the deaths of millions. Following the orders of national leaders, your country's cavalry killed a million Native Americans; Australians exterminated a million Aborigines; Europeans in Africa killed millions; even leaders of a small country like Guatemala have murdered a million Mayans over time, and Pol Pot and the Khmer Rouge slaughtered a million Cambodians. But without the sharp contrast separating 'right' from 'evil,' which is what duality is about, free will would not have any motivation to operate. While each event that causes loss and pain may seem pointless, the energy of compassion, forgiveness, and love that flows from terrifying catastrophes such as war, pestilence, and famine has a worldwide impact that raises the consciousness and vibrational frequency of many people."

My head was a blur as I attempted to get my beliefs out of the way so I could listen. This seemed a totally different concept of duality, in contrast with the usual "equal and polar opposites." He went on, "The energetic ripples from the tragedy of September 11 still reverberate around the world, although not all are compassion, forgiveness, and love. But the emotions of terror and hate were short-lived compared to their intensity at their creation. They would be even less lasting if they were not useful to politicians and bureaucrats who fan the emotional fires that permit money to be spent in any amounts to relieve fears."

It seemed to me that Beelzebub was speaking of the political aftermath, where huge amounts of money were designated for the "war against terrorism." And the American public, including or led by legislators of both political parties, gave their personal power, which means their will to speak their personal truth, to anyone who would "guarantee" their safety and protection from fear and death. In this case, it was President Bush, who took it as his rightful position. But terrorists and terrorism will never be eliminated by war, because war is the ultimate form of terrorism and only perpetuates itself.

Others

Many individuals, as we are informed by daily news reports, act out their dark sides in ways that cause pain and terror. Just like the rest of us, those people die. For those who go to the light, Sylvia Browne *(The Other Side and Back,* 2002*)* reports that they get to the light and are then diverted out a door on the left and immediately return as an unchanged soul for another incarnation. I speculate that there are many soul fragments of this nature that, following the death of their bodies, do not go to the light. They refuse to see the light from the deep, unrelenting fear they will be sent to hell for sins (whatever "sins" may be) or for crimes. Or, they may die violent deaths and be stuck here as entities because of their rage at those who killed them. They look around for a "kindred spirit" to possess, one whose life-force energy they can use and whose actions they can control. Their "life" continues eternally, according to the few "demonic" entities I've spoken to, for whenever the physical body they are with dies, they find another, or wait for that host person to return in a new incarnation. During depossessions, I communicated with one that claimed to have died more than 3,000 years ago, and several that died more than 1,000 years ago. All claimed to have been here continuously, to have experienced religious exorcisms, to have committed murders before and after death; but with all the potential for lying there was no way to distinguish the truth.

In The Spectrum of Consciousness (1979), Ken Wilber said:

Very few of us love our "evil" tendencies. On the contrary, we despise and loathe them, they shame and embarrass us, and we consequently seek not to integrate them but to alienate them…. These negative tendencies of hatred and aggression assume a really violent and evil nature only when we alienate them, only when we separate them from their counterbalancing positive tendencies of love and acceptance and then fling them into the environment where, isolated from their balancing context, they can indeed appear most vicious and destructive. When we incorrectly imagine these demonic aspects to actually exist in the environment — instead of realizing that they exist in us as the necessary counterbalance of our constructive positive tendencies — when we do imagine they exist in the environment, then we react most violently and viciously to this illusory threat, then we are driven into frenzies of frequently brutal crusading, then do we kill "witches" for their own good, start wars to "maintain peace," establish inquisitions to save souls (pp. 206, 207).

My experience has shown that "these demonic aspects" do exist in many people in the form of possessing demons and spirit entities. I believe the solution is to recognize their existence, so "the other" can be separated from "the self." Then, remove them, rather than project the blame for our dark aspects onto others so we can judge ourselves as "right" and those targeted others as "wrong."

Our personal dark side is not a "necessary counterbalance of our constructive positive tendencies," but rather is a collection of aspects — behaviors, actions, and "characters" — of our self that we and others have judged as "bad." With that judgment, we cast those aspects of self into our inner fires of hell for the eternal (as long as we live) mental punishment of guilt and shame. Only when we remember the major dramas of our lives non-judgmentally, and review and re-label the motivations of our behaviors based on the basic human needs (survival, love, recognition, being of service, being free and authentic) rather than the dualities and judgments of "bad" and "wrong," can we hope to forgive our past actions. Then we can integrate our dark side with our conscious self, and become at peace with our self. As Wilbur goes on to say, "We can tame evil only by befriending it, and we simply inflame it by alienating it. Integrated evil becomes quite mellow; projected it becomes quite vicious ..." (p. 208).

Evil as an action of one person against another is supported by possession. Possessing spirits and demons continually subject human conscience to stress, and attempt to undermine it by constantly provoking fear and chaos. Demons have no conscience. The dark forces task them, under threat of severe punishment, to create chaos and disharmony. This is easiest among humans who invite possession through beliefs or greed or desires for power over. Those people are driven by possessing demons and "demonic" spirits to activate the negative attitudes and actions of their repressed dark sides. This is speculated to be one of the causes behind serial murder and serial rape. Those actions (acts of tyranny and power over), along with incest, brutality, and torture, especially of children, are considered to be the darkest evil (defined as morally bad, wicked, sinful).

Summary

Evil is a concept kept alive in our minds by the dark forces that play on people's beliefs, ignorance, fears, and fantasies. The dark forces are controlled by invisible non-human beings on a plane other than the physical. The intent of the dark forces is being carried out on physical Earth by possessing demons and those humans who are controlled by demons.

Fear of evil is triggered and kept alive in people by their personal fantasies of what horrible things their dark sides seem capable of, or of what "bad" it has been capable of in the past, including past lives. The fears are locked in by our judgmental labeling of past events and actions, without understanding human needs, having compassion, or being capable of self-forgiveness. These fears are well maintained by guilt and shame, by the special effects in violent horror movies, by TV newscasts broadcasting horrible catastrophes as if they were ordinary, and by the titillating headlines of scandal sheets. Repressed issues and unresolved fears that people carry from this or past lives are like buttons that can be pushed by the graphic images of these events. Projections of our loved ones, family members, and peer group tend to paralyze us, keeping us from seeking help.

The New Spirituality

In the new spirituality people will be aware of the full capabilities and history of human beings at their darkest and lightest levels. All past history of the various cultures will be remembered in the "collective conscious" of all; no acts, regardless of how evil, will be denied or buried in the subconscious. Acts of war will not be required because the horrors and excesses of war will be remembered.

In the fifth and higher dimensions to which we are ascending, leadership of a religion or country or corporation will not provide a temptation because at the higher frequencies of vibration anyone will be able to manifest whatever they desire. The dark forces will no longer attract those who would trade away their souls for material "stuff." The only attractions will be the journeys and paths that lead most directly to the divine light of unconditional love as illusions and veils drop away and people awaken to their spiritual true self.

The archangels, spirit teachers, and God are all available to help when we make the request. The appeal for help must be made before help will be given. The final chapter illustrates reasons for possession that I have discovered during the past several years.

Chapter Fourteen

Purposes of Possession

In the desert, The Adversary (Sa-Tan) tempted Jesus to perform miracles to show his greatness, and to kneel down and pay homage to the dark being in return for power over all the empires of the world. But Jesus said, "Get out of here, Satan! Remember, it is written that 'You are to pay homage to the Lord your God, and you are to revere him alone'" (Mt. 4:10). Thus, the adversarial and tempting force, whether giant demon, Satan, or Beelzebub, went away, as there was no "doorway" for it to enter. Jesus showed the forces of darkness, and the world, that he was resolute in his character and steadfast in his resolve to continue his mission, his purpose. Again, he provided a model that shows us how to repel The Adversary of our lives.

And that is my understanding of the greater purpose, and power, of lesser demons, giant demons, fallen angels, and the dark forces. Like Jesus going to the desert, we humans announce our intention at various times to be tested, tempted, and tormented. At times, the intention does not seem fully conscious or fully developed. Like a half-finished painting, part is complete and the remainder consists of sketches, doodles, and blank space. Then, when The Adversary arrives on the scene, we protest, "Wait. I am not ready!" But interestingly enough, spirit does not register negatives that follow the declarative "I am."

"I am ready" is an individual's declaration to divine spirit of an intention to change. And some spiritual being in heaven is instantly alerted to begin proceedings, synchronous events, to ensure that the intention or prayer is supported. What follows is not necessarily pretty: tests and initiations can include loss of job and physical handicap; temptation includes opportunities to lie, cheat, and steal, all in some attempt to create a self-identity that does not have all the cracks and flaws that our perception (our mirror) and beliefs show us to have. Torments include pestilence (cancer), plague (AIDS), death (loved ones), and war (threat of nuclear annihilation).

Demons are the front-line "soldiers" to test, tempt, and torment to be the human adversary. They are the dark-side teachers, teaching us about our shadow self, our wild animal self, and our lower physical soul, all of which we try to deny. Demons are the drivers. Sometimes they actively drive human minds and actions toward involvement with the dark forces to produce evil acts. They attempt to separate light beings from their inherent connection with God. Other times they simply and passively block people from the inner knowing of their soul's life purpose by keeping them fearful of exploring the world.

Those who give in to their fears or are seduced by the tempting promises of demons are granted the opportunity to explore the darkness of their dark side, to align with whatever are the dark forces, to develop their character in the darkest way they choose. Who are we to judge? We do not know the spiritual life contracts of others. We do not know what sacred path they are on. The serial killer, the terrorist, the rapist, the bully, the child-killing mother or father, the sexually abusive priest or minister, all are children of God, all here for some divine purpose unknown to us. And we are not their divine judge. Each person does that for him- or herself following death. But the horrific actions of some of these individuals certainly keep alive the concept that people are evil.

The God-directed purpose of Beelzebub is to provide for humanity everything that he can create in the way of testing, temptation, and adversity that will help bring out the best of our true selves. He does that through contrast: contrast between dark and light, contrast between pain and joy, contrast between misery and bliss. He maintains the duality of third-dimensional misery.

Information from Beelzebub and other spiritual beings indicates that the original cause of evil in the world had an extraterrestrial source of reptilian nature that was likely the Nephilim. They came to Earth following the little-known Dark Force that flows through the universe as a continuous but migrating sinuous ribbon or stream of dark energy and power (from a personal channeling by Crystal Down Morris, 2002). They found here the resources they were searching for: minerals and human emotions; and they mined both, even taking the "lesser" demons as a source of fuel and power. They warred with the Giants and the Fallen Angels and the Adams, and probably entered into breeding experiments with humans. But all of that has been written by others.

Adversity is the true teacher of life in this third-dimensional world. The greatest growth in character and personal resolve, or the greatest destruction, which provides increased margin for growth, occurs during adversity.

Suffice it to say that before we come into each lifetime, we write out in our sacred life contracts what types of physical third-dimensional challenges and adversity we desire as tests to spur the development of our souls. What we do not know is when they will happen, and what they will feel like. As I said once in the agony of a kidney-stone attack, "Why would anyone do this to himself?" Lifetime after lifetime, each of us may face the same challenges provided by the same demons, until we remember who we are: a spirit having a physical experience, a piece of God out on the leading edge of human consciousness; and find the way to take up our power to be the person we came to be.

The New Spirituality

In the new spirituality we are creating in this transforming world, we do not need the personal experience of adversity, temptation of power or money, pain, suffering, and fear in order to know who we are not. All those experiences exist within the collective consciousness that is available to each of us. Therefore, we no longer have to experience them to understand them. Although we may need to be reminded, we know that they existed in the world's "then." We can choose in the "now" to create a new being: "Pain and suffering and fear are who I am not. I am that which I am." Love, joy, and passion for life can then fill our existence.

Bibliography

Amorth, Gabriele. *An Exorcist Tells His Story*. San Francisco: Ignatius Press, 1999.

Baldwin, William J. *Spirit Releasement Therapy: A Technique Manual*. Terra Alta, WV: Headline Books, 1995.

Berne, Eric. *What Do You Say After You Say Hello?: The Psychology of Human Destiny*. New York: Bantam Books, 1973.

Blatty, William Peter. *The Exorcist*. New York: Harper and Row, 1971.

Bly, Robert. *A Little Book on the Human Shadow*. William Booth, ed. San Francisco: Harper, 1988.

Bowker, John. *The Complete Bible Handbook*. New York: DK Publishing, 1998.

Brennan, Barbara Ann, *Hands of Light: A Guide to Healing Through the Human Energy Field*. New York: Bantam, 1995.

Browne, Sylvia. *The Nature of Good and Evil*. Carlsbad, CA: Hay House, 2001.

Browne, Sylvia. *Conversations With the Other Side*. Carlsbad, CA: Hay House, 2002.

Browne, Sylvia. *The Other Side and Back*. Carlsbad, CA: Hay House, 2002.

Carroll, Lee. *Kryon – The End Times: New Information for Personal*

Peace. San Diego, CA: Kryon Writings, 1993.

Connolly, David. *In Search of Angels: A Celestial Sourcebook for Beginning Your Journey.* New York: Perigee Books, 1993.

Cousins, David. *A Handbook for Lightworkers.* Jean Prince, ed. Dartmouth: Barton House, 1993.

Cuneo, Michael W. *American Exorcism: Expelling Demons in the Land of Plenty.* New York, Doubleday, 2001.

Dowling, Levi H. *The Aquarian Gospel of Jesus the Christ.* Marina del Rey, CA: DeVorss, 1997.

Eliade, Mircea. *Shamanism: Archaic Techniques of Ecstasy.* Trans. William R. Trask. Princeton: Princeton University Press, 1964.

Fiore, Edith. *You Have Been Here Before: A Psychologist Looks at Past Lives.* New York: Ballantine Books, 1978.

Fiore, Edith. *The Unquiet Dead: A Psychologist Treats Spirit Possession.* New York: Ballantine Books, 1987.

Ford, Debbie. *The Dark Side of the Light Chasers: Reclaiming Your Power, Creativity, Brilliance, and Dreams.* New York: Riverhead Books, 1998.

Furst, Jeffrey. *Edgar Cayce's Story of Jesus.* New York: Berkley Medallion Books, 1968.

Green, Glenda. *Love Without End: Jesus Speaks…* Sedona: Spiritis Publishing, 1999.

Harner, Michael. *The Way of the Shaman.* 3rd ed. San Francisco: Harper, 1990.

Herman, Ronna. *The Golden Promise: Messages of Hope and Inspiration from Archangel Michael.* Mt. Shasta, CA: Mt. Shasta Light Publishing, 2000.

Hillman, James. *The Soul's Code: In Search of Character and Calling.* New York: Warner Books, 1996.

Illustrated Dictionary and Concordance of the Bible. Ed. Geoffrey Wigoder. Jerusalem: The Jerusalem Publishing House, 1986.

Jenkins, Philip. *Pedophiles and Priests: Anatomy of a Contemporary Crisis*. New York: Oxford University Press, 2001.

Jung, C. G. *Memories, Dreams, Reflections*. Rev. ed. Trans. Richard and Clara Winston. Ed. Aniela Jaffe. New York: Vintage Books, 1989.

Josephus. *Antiquities of the Jews: Book VIII*. The Bible Library CD-Rom. Oklahoma City: Ellis Enterprises, 2000.

Josephus. *Jewish Wars: VII*. The Bible Library CD-Rom. Oklahoma City: Ellis Enterprises, 2000.

Knight, Kevin. *The Catholic Encyclopedia, Volume IV*. Online Edition: Newadvent.org/cathen, 1999, 2003.

Koltuv, Barbara Black. *The Book of Lilith*. York Beach Maine: Nicolas-Hays, Inc., 1986.

Kubler-Ross, Elisabeth. *On Death and Dying*. New York: Macmillan Publishing, 1969.

Kubler-Ross, Elisabeth. *Death: The Final Stage of Growth*. New York: Simon and Schuster, 1975.

Lamsa, George. *The Modern New Testament from Aramaic*. New York: The Aramaic Bible Society, Inc., 2002.

MacNutt, Francis. *Deliverance from Evil Spirits: A Practical Manual*. Grand Rapids: Chosen Books, 1995.

Marciniak, Barbara. *Earth:Pleaidian Keys to the Living Library*. Ed. Tera L. Thomas. Rochester, VT: Bear and Co., 1994.

Martin, Malachi. *Hostage to the Devil: The Possession and Exorcism of Five Contemporary Americans*. San Francisco: Harper, 1976.

Maurey, Eugene. *Exorcism: How to Clear at a Distance a Spirit Possessed Person*. Atglen, PA, Whitford Press, 1988.

Miller, Robert J., ed. *The Complete Gospels: Annotated Scholars Version*. San Francisco: Harper, 1994.

Mitchell, Roy. *The Exile of the Soul: The Case for Two Souls in the Constitution of Every Man*. Ed. John L. Davenport. Buffalo: Prometheus Books, 1983.

Modi, Shakuntala. *Remarkable Healings: A Psychiatrist Discovers Unsuspected Roots of Mental and Physical Illness*. Charlottesville, VA: Hampton Roads Publishing Co., 1997.

Myss, Caroline. *Anatomy of the Spirit: The Seven Stages of Power and Healing*. New York: Seven Rivers Press, 1996.

Myss, Caroline. *Sacred Contracts*. New York: Harmony Books, 2001.

Myss, Caroline. *Why People Don't Heal and How They Can*. New York: Harmony Books, 1997.

Oesterreich, T. K. *Possession: Demoniacal and Other Among Primitive Races in Antiquity, the Middle Ages, and Modern Times*. Trans. By D. Ibberson. New York: University Books, 1966.

Pagels, Elaine. *The Origin of Satan*. New York: Vintage Books, 1995.

Peck, M. Scott. *People of the Lie: The Hope for Healing Human Evil*. New York: Simon and Schuster, 1983.

Perkins, John, *The World Is as You Dream It: Shamanic Teachings from the Amazon and Andes*. Rochester, VT: Destiny Books, 1994.

Prophet, Elizabeth Clare. *Fallen Angels and the Origins of Evil: Why Church Fathers Supressed the Book of Enoch and Its Startling Revelations*. Corwin Springs, MT: Summit University Press, 2000.

Reed, Henry. *Edgar Cayce: On Channeling Your Higher Self*. New York: Warner Books, 1989.

Rother, Steve. *Re-member: A Handbook for Human Evolution*. Poway, CA: Lightworker, 2000.

Rother, Steve. *Welcome Home*. Carlsbad, CA: Lightworker, 2002.

Rudwin, Maximillian. *The Devil in Legend and Literature*. La Salle, IL: Open Court Publishing, 1959.

Sagan, Samuel. *Entity Possession: Freeing the Energy Body of Negative Influences*. Rochester, VT: Destiny Books, 1997.

Saraydarian, Torkom. *Battling Dark Forces: A Guide to Psychic Self-Defense*. Sedona: New Vision Publishing, 1998.

Sitchin, Zecharia. *The 12ᵗʰ Planet: Book I of the Earth Chronicles*. New York: Avon Books, 1976.

Sitchin, Zecharia. *Divine Encounters: A Guide to Visions, Angels, and other Emissaries*. New York: Avon Books, 1995.

Smith, William. *The New Smith's Bible Dictionary*. Rev. Reuel G. Lemmons. New York: Doubleday and Co., 1966.

Stanford, Peter. *The Devil: A Biography*. New York: Henry Holt, 1996.

Tyndale House Publishers Staff, ed. *Holy Bible: New Living Translation*. Wheaton, IL: Tyndale House Publishers, 1996.

Virtue, Doreen. *Healing With the Angels: How the Angels Can Assist You in Every Area of Your Life*. Carlsbad, CA: Hay House, 1999.

Wagner, Doris M. *How to Cast Out Demons: A Guide to the Basics*. Ventura, CA: Gospel Light, 2000.

Walsch, Neale Donald. *Conversations With God Book I: An Uncommon Dialogue*. New York: Penguin Putnam, 1996.

Webster's II New College Dictionary. New York: Houghton Mifflin Co., 2001.

Whyte, H. A. Maxwell. *A Manual On Exorcism*. Monroeville, PA: Whitaker House, 1974.

Whyte, H. A. Maxwell. *Casting Out Demons*. New Kensington, PA: Whitaker House, 1973.

Wilber, Ken. *The Spectrum of Consciousness*. Wheaton, IL: The Theosophical Publishing House, 1979.

Williamson, Marianne. *A Return to Love*. New York: Harper Trade, 1992.

Wise, Michael O., Martin Abegg, and Edward Cook. *The Dead Sea Scrolls: A New Translation*. San Francisco: Harper, 1996.

Appendix A

Use of a Pendulum

Practitioners need methods of divination to answer questions for and about themselves and clients. Valid information can come from intuition, clairvoyant abilities, runes, bones, meditation, shamanic journeying to spirit teachers, and inner journeying to higher self. I use dowsing with a pendulum, as described in the next section, as a quick method of divination where the information is derived from a higher source.

There are many books on the history and use of the pendulum, including *Techniques of Pendulum Dowsing* (Bill Cox, 1977), and *Pendulum Power* (Nielsen and Polansky, 1977). Cox says that the ancient Egyptians and Polynesians worked with the pendulum. The Chinese began to use pendulums at least 6,000 years ago, and historical records from ancient Greece describe its use as well.

I have found that 85 to 90 percent of all people can use the pendulum, regardless of their beliefs about psychic or paranormal abilities. A pendulum is any weighted object on the end of a three- to six-inch piece of string, cord, or fine chain (a doubled chain, as in a necklace or key chain will work, but is not as precise as a single strand).

Place the string over the outside tip of the index finger with the weight suspended about three inches below. Place the thumb over the string to hold it in place, the thumbnail facing up. The first question to ask of a new pendulum is: "What is my 'Yes' direction?" The pendulum will move in one of four directions: back and forth, side to side, or describe circles in either direction. When you have determined the Yes direction, then ask: "What is my 'No' direction?" If the movements are small and unclear, practice for up to three months may be required while asking for larger movements from the pendulum.

When asking about the presence of parasitic beings, the questions are:

1. Do I have a spirit entity attached?
2. Do I have a lesser demon attached?
3. Do I have a giant demon attached?
4. Do I have a shape-shifting giant demon attached?
5. Do I have a fallen angel attached?
6. Do I have a dark ET* attached?
7. Am I clear of all parasitic beings?

---

* Subject of another book.

Appendix B

Practitioner Preparation

Many of us growing up may feel that we have no inherent talents and that we must learn everything from a teacher. Recently, I have felt that there are six major aspects of myself, due to challenges in my early childhood, that allow me to be excellent at depossession and exorcism. While I was growing up, each of these was a cross to bear; a source of personal shame to a degree. Having had to learn to see the gold nugget in each, I describe them so those of you who are interested in this work may look with compassion and forgiveness on some of your own wrongly judged talents.

Listener: I love to hear people's stories, out of curiosity for how they got to be the way they are. I didn't learn to talk about myself until late in life. This listening and curiosity carried over to the area of what spirits are and how they got where they are. By now, through great teachings from clients, spirits, and demons, I have learned how to redirect and cut off stories that have the intent of misleading me. Of course, I've found that I need to stay open to the possibility that where they want to go may be the best place.

Peacemaker: As a child, I became a peacemaker between my parents, intervening in my mother's pain and sadness, and providing a target for my father's rage. Later, as a therapist, I learned better ways — not taking on pain and not being the target — that helped with spirits and demons. I believe that one of an exorcist's tasks is to help clients return to an original state of peace, a state of grace. Many clients experience great relief when they find they can talk with me about "wyrd stuff." When I phone to ask how they are the morning after I do a healing exorcism, many clients, say they feel peaceful for the first time in a long time.

Truth seeker: In my extended family of origin, truth was so elusive a quality that it could seldom be found. Secrets were the usual currency; denial and placation — "Everything's all right," — were the norm to "keep from hurting people's feelings." But all of that was "crazy-making." I became an avid and somewhat obsessive seeker of the truth, about others, about life, about other realms, and later, about myself. Now I rely on divine guidance rather than on my ego for which questions to ask when. An effective exorcist must be free of myths, prejudices, and judgments about evil, devils, demons, hell, and Heaven. He or she must be able to speak only the truth to spirits and demons, without resorting to bluffs, lies, and power over, which are the resorts of sorcerers and exorcisms of the Catholic Church. Unless one has authority over them, demons tell lies as a matter of course. They lie about everything! For this and other reasons, I rarely speak with them.

Unafraid: Much of my life, I considered (judged) myself a coward: I lived in terror of when my father might explode into crazy rage; I was scared of when the bullies at school might hit me, afraid of being ridiculed, and afraid to appear "stupid." I was scared of members of my therapy group in prison, panicked by the black phantom that stalked my young-adult dreams, and terrified of when I might explode in anger and hurt someone. Slowly, by finding that my fears were caused by my belief that I was alone and without support and love, I went into and through fear, in a many-year process, and came out the other side as who I now am. As my fears were displaced by love from and for myself, rage and hate and other negative, fear-based emotions loosened the stranglehold that I had given them. Exorcists may encounter threats of physical harm from demons and spirits. Nonetheless, they must be capable of continuing their work in a state of grace, rather than reacting in a fight-or-flight manner. Along with awareness of any fear that may be triggered, they must understand that fear is an emotion that will pass if they don't hold on to it; that their training and experience will carry them through, similar to martial artists (courtesy of Dan Millman, *The Peaceful Warrior Training*, 1996).

Stubborn: One of the qualities I appreciate in myself, probably helped by my Taurean sun sign, is my good way of hanging in, even when the way is difficult, dangerous, or filled with unknowns. Some call this stubbornness. Others find different ways of getting similar jobs done, but there aren't many others doing this particular work.

Sleep Inducing. I used to be embarrassed about my boring voice, my ability to put people to sleep in the talks I gave. My teacher at the time gave up on trying to have me use humor and a greater range of voice tone — which came effortlessly to him — to add "life" to my verbal work. It was partly fear of talking and showing myself in public, but partly, it was my natural talent for hypnotizing people that was coming alive. Now I can assist a wide range of people to deep levels of relaxation, where, among other things, they are able to understand what "doorway" they opened that first allowed entry to spirits or demons.

Basic Training and Experience

To be an effective practitioner in this field, the world of the spiritual must be known, not as it is usually taught by religion, but as is known by the esoteric and shamanic. Then, the practitioner knows with some certainty what spirits and demons are, why they are here, and where they need to go upon removal from a person. Also, a practitioner must have some ability to "see," "feel," or "know" the presence of spirits and demons attached to a person's body-mind, and be able to confirm when they are gone. Lastly, to do this work a practitioner requires assistance, power, and authority from a higher spiritual power. Anyone who attempts to do this work using his or her own physical power and authority, or that of the dark forces, is both in the realm of sorcery and asking for a very challenging lesson.

Basic shamanic training, consisting of an introductory journey workshop and plus advanced training in a death-and-dying workshop, provides an excellent foundation — not as a shaman, but as a more conscious person and one who can relate to the spiritual world. A resulting working relationship with a spirit teacher and helper(s) will provide support and personal power. Working relationships with the archangels and the angelic beings, or with additional spirit teachers, can be accomplished through other training.

The basic certification course in hypnotherapy, or better yet, advanced training in clinical hypnotherapy, provides much more than a degree in psychology. It is an excellent method of gaining understanding and experience with the workings of the conscious and subconscious mind, understanding of the inner child, the formation of habits and beliefs, suggestion, and healing. Hypnosis is how most parents teach their children; therefore, it is highly effective as the method for "unlearning." Past-life and pre-life regression are very useful in my practice, as is knowledge of methods for healing past lives from the point of the present. Alchemical schools are recommended for their use of spirit teachers and helpers during hypnotherapy work.

For this work, or any other deep-process work with another person, practitioners owe it to their clients to be emotionally and mentally stable during events that have potential to generate fear and high stress. It is important that practitioners have such spiritual help and support as the angelic realm provides. With unconditional love, their help is freely offered for the asking. Books and workshops by Doreen Virtue (*Healing With The Angels*, 1999) provide excellent methods for working with the angels as healing partners.

Appendix C
Methods of Depossession

This section is for those intending to engage in this work.

Exorcism Using Dowsing Techniques

Bill Finch (*The Pendulum and Possession*, 1975) and the late Rev. Eugene Maurey (*Exorcism*, 1988), wrote detailed methods of exorcism using the pendulum, psychic ability, and a scripted spoken command. I modified Maurey's work and used these methods into the early 1990s, asking the questions below, which I had written out on a prepared form. I used a pendulum to obtain my answers (see the previous section for suggestions of pendulum use).

Is this person possessed by spirit entities?
"Give me an indication, on the chart, of the number of negative spirit entities within this person." The chart is a radial arc shaped like a parachute, with numbers from 1 to 10 spread evenly across the top, connected by radial lines to a common point below. When placed at the apex or common point, the pendulum will swing along the correct line in answer.

"Give me an indication (on a different chart), of the strongest possessing negative entity." This chart is similar in shape, but evenly spread across the canopy, right to left, are the numbers 1, 2, 3, 5, 10, 20, 25, and 30. For those who prefer to work in metaphors, the numbers seem to equate with the following social roles: "victim," "persecuted," "pawn," "passive," "bully," "persecutor," "sorcerer," and "demonic."

"Do I have permission of the person's higher self to clear this person of spirit entities?" Often, the request comes from a family member or loved one, not from the person, so receiving permission is an absolute requirement before performing any healing work.

Once permission is obtained, the following scripts for exorcism, which I modified from Maurey's work, can be read aloud. The practitioner needs a working connection with the archangel Michael, trust in his or her own psychic abilities, and faith that the process works. This is one of the safest methods of removing spirit entities, because the practitioner is not in close proximity, especially with those with the relative negative strength of −20, −25, and −30. Among those spirits might be those without social conscience, that have performed abusive acts, murder or worse, during and after their physical lives. Some of those possessed by these spirit entities might be in jail, prison, or mental institutions. Using the same chart as in No. 3, the operator can ask, "What is the strongest possessing negative entity that I can work with at this time?" Higher numbers can be referred to another practitioner, or kept on file while amassing more experience.

The following scripts, in boldface type, are read aloud:

Statement of the Intent to Clear (using a loving voice):
I am asking for help from the archangel Michael and the

spirit helpers and guardian angel of [client's name]. Please address yourselves to the spirit entities within the body, mind, and soul of [client's name], those around him or her, in the home and at the workplace, and prepare to escort them to the place they need to go.

Statement for Spirit Release
(use a firm voice of command from the heart):

I now address the spirit entities and any harmful energies in and around [client's name]. You are caught between levels of this physical universe, on the other side of the veil of death. You may not remember the death of your physical body. I assure you that you died, and I am aware that you may have experienced fear and suffering during that death. You may now let go of those feelings. [Pause.] I am aware that you feel very much alive while in the body of another person, but you do not belong there. You are causing trouble to the life of the person you are with, as well as trouble to yourself. You deserve to go to a better place where there is love and healing, and you can be among your loved ones who have gone on before you. Do you remember your mother's name, or your grandmother's? [Pause.]

For this last part, hold your pendulum with the thought-request of "Show me a positive direction until the spirit entity is home at the light." Once the pendulum movement begins, speak the following last part more rapidly because events move quickly:

Now, at this moment, you will sense or see angelic beings and your spirit guides next to you, along with the hands of your loved ones reaching to you from the light. You may

trust them and their love. They will take you by the hand
and lead you where you need to go. As you reach up your
hand and take theirs, reach back and take the hands of those
spirits behind you to help them all on their way. Go now!
[Monitor the pendulum motion until it stops, and then check
that the client is cleared.]

Your can record your results on a form that could have the
following at the bottom:
Cleared [Yes / No] **Date / Time** _____
Repeated [Yes / No] **Date / Time** _____
To me, more important than recording information on forms
is the release of the spirit entity to the light and the healing of the
person. This method can be attempted with demons; however,
the script would need to be modified, and demons, particularly
of the giant and shape-shifting varieties, might disregard the
commands.

Depossession with Hypnosis

Hypnosis is used to assist the client (and attached being) into
a relaxed, altered state of consciousness in which the spirit or
demon talks with the healer through the voice of the client (client
as medium). Again, a working relationship with the archangel
Michael for help and protection is essential.

After twenty years as a clinical hypnotherapist, I found that
little or nothing in the form of hypnotic induction was required
to bring a client to the relaxed state in which the removal of
an attached spirit could be accomplished. Probably, my soft,
soporific, relaxing voice is my most useful tool for this and other
healing work. I maintain focus on the client's breathing until it

becomes relaxed. Sometimes I use a count from 1 to 10 (or 10 to 1), with the suggestion that the client will "relax to a deeper level with each number that I count, until at 10 you will be at the deepest level of relaxation possible today." At most, a few minutes are required for the necessary stage of relaxation.

To determine the presence of spirit entities, and for yes-or-no answers to other simple questions, the hypnotized client can use finger signals (*The Unquiet Dead*, p. 9). The relaxed client is asked which finger is his Yes finger, and which his No finger, and the suggestion is made that he will respond with those fingers in answer to questions. But, as Fiore points out, spirit entities can attempt to manipulate the fingers to mislead the healer.

The "depossession technique" transcript by Fiore (pp. 130–33) can be read verbatim as she recommends, or the transcript of the dowsing method can be read, to move spirit entities on to the light. A transcript is useful in cases where the spirit entity is resistant due to shyness or rebellion. If verbal dialogue is desired, the spirit entity may be talked with as detailed in the following sections, through a medium or face to face.

William Baldwin has provided detailed methodology and case histories for use of hypnosis in dialogue with spirit entities and demons (*Spirit Releasement Therapy*, 1992). Baldwin, a hypnotherapist, is a student of Fiore, and his book is thorough, supported by detailed case transcripts and backed by a full training program for interested professionals. Baldwin's descriptions of demons and their abilities is excellent.

Modi's book, *Remarkable Healings* (1997), is filled with clinical case histories of depossessions of spirit entities and demons.

Depossession with a Medium

A medium is any person who knowingly offers his or her voice for temporary use by a spirit entity in order for a spirit to be heard and depossession to be performed. Some mediums, through their own will or effort, enter states ranging from light to deep trance. Others function in unaltered states of mind. Usually, the practitioner acts as a negotiator to speak with the spirit entity talking through the medium. But, as I have been told by the shamanic healer-medium who was my partner for three years, there are mediums who perform both the role of medium and healer-negotiator with the spirit entity.

As I learned from my partner, mediums can be of great help in depossessions if they have clairvoyant ability to see a spirit entity with a client (its human host) and see whether it is releasing from the client or is hesitant or fearful; if they can assure the spirit, through thought-transfer, that there is no trick and that no harm will come; if they can see the approach of a possessing spirit after it releases from a client, and can allow the spirit to merge its energy and vibration with their vocal cords and so use their voices.

Brazilian Spiritist Depossession

I haven't used the following method, but, in 1997, as a volunteer "subject" at a workshop hosted by the Foundation for Shamanic Studies, I experienced it during a depossession by three healers of the Brazilian Spiritist Church. They created a formal setting in which everyone sat around a table, keeping their hands on the table and their feet flat on the floor. The healers, who were shamanic or psychic healers, sat at one end of the table; the client (I) sat near them and across from the designated medium. Others filled in around the table, and additional people sat in an outer circle around the table. The table and chairs were spiritually wired together in a circuit. Prayers were said and spirit helpers were called in. The client opened a holy text to a page that was then read by one of the healers to establish the theme of the depossession. Everyone in the circle was requested to remain silent until after the first spirit entity had made its appearance through the medium. In an atmosphere of love and truth, the healers negotiated verbally with the spirit entity, in a dialogue similar to the recommended twelve steps presented later in this appendix. Following depossession of that spirit entity, and guidance to the light by the healers, anyone in the circle of onlookers could become the medium for additional spirits until all were released from the client. When anyone in the outer circle gave voice to a spirit entity, many becoming mediums for the first time, they were invited to the table to complete the depossession. The work continued until all the spirit entities were cleared from the client. This method would work well for a trained circle processing many clients during a meeting. However, demons were not worked with, and it is not for the solo practitioner.

Shamanic Journey Depossession

In a typical situation, a client first visits a shamanic practitioner to ask for healing. Usually, a divination of the root cause of the client's issues is undertaken: the practitioner makes a shamanic journey to his spirit teacher or helper to find what healing is required. He may be told to perform a depossession of the spirit entities and/or demons attached to the client. In my practice, I usually do this first, to remove any energy or entity that would interfere with other healing work. The spirits may recommend other shamanic, holistic, and/or allopathic (M.D.) healing for later.

As my spirit teacher taught me, the journey to connect with the client's spirit/soul is conducted in the Middle World, in the here and now of spiritual reality. The practitioner will enter into an altered state of consciousness — through drumming, rattling, chanting, toning, dancing, or some other creative method — where she can "walk in two worlds."

The mission of the shamanic journey is to meet with the spirit/the soul of the client. Therefore, the practitioner asks his power animal, spirit teacher, or angelic being to take him on a journey in the Middle World, to a meeting with the soul of the client (by name and location). The meeting can be held in a place known to the practitioner, such as his magic garden. The time that it takes to reach there in the journey may take a few seconds to a minute (two minutes would "seem" like a long journey).

The appearance of the client's soul will not be known in advance, and may range from the way the client looks sitting in front of the practitioner in ordinary reality, to a much heavier, darker form, or possibly a shimmer of light approximately the shape and size of a human. The form of the client's soul is an important feature, as regards his or her spiritual health.

Spirit Entities: At this moment, it is the spirit entity or entities attached to the client that are of prime importance. The appearance of the possessing spirit entity is not known in advance. It is usually smaller, as if shrunken. Often, it is found hiding behind the client's soul, where it may be difficult to see or entirely distinguish, as the merger of energy between the client and attached spirit entity can range from nearly complete to nearly separate.

The spirit entity is asked, in a kind, loving voice, as a parent might use with a child, to release its hold on the client and step out and speak with the practitioner, as in the following: "I ask you to release your hold on (client's name) and step out here and speak with me. Please tell me your name." Usually, it's that simple. It seems that possessing spirits trust other spirits (such as those of journeying shamans) that appear before them.

Commonly, the spirit entity can be better identified as to sex and age when it is out in open view. The introductory remarks are to begin the dialogue, which, to observers, is silent. Then, the "twelve-step" depossession sequence in the following section can be used.

Sorcerer Entities: Some spirit entities that were sorcerers in a past life hold hundreds of fragments of the souls of others, and may resist returning them, for that was their power during their lifetimes, and they may have found ways to continue using that power after their deaths. An angelic being may be asked to explain to sorcerer spirits why they need to return the stolen parts. I have overheard some of the conversations; in a no-nonsense approach by the angelic beings, they say something like: "The time for your games is finished. Do what the man tells you." The former practitioners of dark magic respond quickly to that. Following this agreement, the practitioner — without knowing who they are — calls on the guardian angels of all whose soul fragments the sorcerer holds. They instantly appear, take their respective parts, and depart.

Demonic Entities: The practitioner may encounter a strong-willed demonic-type spirit entity that considers itself a demon due to criminal or immoral events during life. It may refuse to come out and speak, hanging back and attempting to hide from the practitioner, pushing other spirit entities forward to fool him or her. As described in more detail in Chapter Seven, much of what these particular entities say may be lies intended to spread confusion and gain control. I have dialogued with such entities and found it of little reward.

Therefore, when I have identified the presence of a demonic-type spirit entity that refuses to come out and speak with me and give me a true name, I call on the archangel Michael and make this request: "Please place a light-filled bubble over this spirit entity, shrink it tight, and take it where it needs to go." The bubble appears similar to the one that transported Glinda, the good witch, Dorothy's fairy godmother in *The Wonderful Wizard of Oz.*

Possessing Demons: During a shamanic journey, possessing demons may be seen attached to the client. The "lesser" demons may be seen as small gray-to-black blobs attached to the client's energy body or to a spirit entity attached to the client's body. The back of the neck appears to be a favored spot. The archangel Michael taught me the following way to "handle" demons in the shamanic journey method of depossession (months before teaching me the methods of exorcism described in Chapter Eleven). In summary, I was told to call on the archangel Michael and the Mighty Warriors of Light on Earth — special angelic warrior beings that deal directly with demons — and request help by saying, "I call on the archangel Michael and the Mighty Warriors of Light for help with removing this demon. Please place a light-filled bubble around this demon, shrink it tight, and take it to the nearest river and immerse it in the water. Please take all "watcher" demons to the river and immerse them in the water." The Giant

Demons, described in Chapters Nine and Ten, can appear in many forms, but the one thing they have in common is a very large appearance. I recommend that the Giant Demons, when encountered, be encapsulated in a "super bubble" filled with light, per information in Chapter Eleven.

When all the steps of the next section have been followed, when all spirit entities have been taken, psychopomped, to the light (explained fully in Chapter Eight), the demons to where they need to go, where they can cause no further harm, the practitioner can return from the journey. The client is checked by psychic vision or pendulum to see that he or she is cleared, and that there is no "free-floating" spirit entity (one that can move freely from one member of a family to another, or within a group, causing anger or violence) that has shifted to some other family member, or hidden so as to cause trouble later). This work can be done equally well at a distance.

Twelve Steps of Depossession

Following are the twelve steps of a depossession of spirit entities, based on methods described by Edith Fiore (*The Unquiet Dead,*1987), and which I modified during four years of practice in methods of hypnosis, with a medium, face to face, and with the shamanic journey. In the year 2000, as I became aware of demons, as distinct from "demonic" spirit entities, the archangel Michael advised me that I no longer needed verbal dialogue with spirits or demons, either for myself or the client (though I still dialogue with clients' dead relatives), and that I could call on the angelic beings to remove the possessing spirits and demons and request that they take them to the light or wherever they needed to go.

Healers, using any one of the previous methods of depossession, can call on whatever spiritual help and power they are accustomed to working with or think they need. The work is done — *must be done* — in a gentle but firm, caring voice, and in an environment of impeccability, truth, love, fearlessness, compassion, respect for spirits and clients, and the desire to be of service.

Although not numbered, this introductory first step is essential: help the client relax, instructing her to breath deeply and gently several times (watch her abdomen to see that the breathing is in that area; if it is only high up in the chest, she is not relaxed). Have her close her eyes and imagine herself "surrounded and filled with the divine white light of unconditional love." Then suggest that she will be able to allow her ego to move aside so the work can go on. There is no intent to hypnotize, though the client may enter an altered state of consciousness on her own.

The possessing spirit entities will begin listening attentively. Address them to reduce their possible fears. Give them verbal assurance that no tricks or traps are planned, that there is no hell anywhere (other than in the mind), that they will not be hurt or cease to exist by leaving the person they are connected with, and that they will have the opportunity to go to a world of light and love, where the loved ones and family members who have gone before will be waiting to greet them. There they can be healed of all pain and suffering experienced on Earth. It is imperative that you, the practitioner, believe everything you are saying.

The intent of step number 1 is to make verbal contact with one of the possessing spirit entities, through any of the previously described direct methods:

    a. Face to face, with hypnosis, the client acting as the medium to provide a voice for the spirit;

b. With a medium, or

c. Through shamanic journey. Once contact is made, which may take between two and fifteen minutes, continue the verbal dialogue through the remaining steps:

1. Ask the spirit entity to speak with you and tell you its name. In a soft, soporific monotone, continually call out to the entity, referring to it as a "confused being" or "lonely being" and asking for its name, until you are answered.

2. Ask the spirit entity the last event it remembers from when it had a physical body. Do not allow the entity to go off on tangents in telling its story, unless there is reason to find out the age at death, the year of death, and whether the entity is a relative, friend, or lover of the client).

3. Take the spirit entity step by painful step through the death of its physical body, asking for elaboration on de-tails of the emotions felt at the moment of death ("And then what happened? And then what happened?"), until the entity reports that it has separated from the physical body. Keep it at the scene of death, however; do not let it run away.

4. Have the spirit entity acknowledge that it is separated from the body, that it is in another location from the body, and that the body is dead. Do not tell the entity that it is dead, or it may remain in denial and refuse to go along with your guidance.

5. At this time, a healing of all unresolved emotions held by the spirit entity about its death may be completed. The unresolved emotions and personal conflicts held at death become the issues that are carried forward, as karma, to the next life. The entity can be asked to open the doors to its heart (the place of storage for all relationship emotions),

and its belly (the place of storage for all personal emotions), and allow all stored emotions related to the death of the physical body to be released back into the physical body there in view of the spirit entity. Personal conflicts are always resolved by forgiveness, not of any horrible and abusive actions that may have occurred, but of a person's humanness in not knowing better ways of being. This clearing process allows the spirit entity to come into the now, where it will be more open to the offered choice of going to the light. The spirit may suddenly be able to see angelic beings around it and know the reasons for what occurred during its life.

6. Optionally, at this point, you could ask the entity questions about its life: when it was born, when and how it died, what attracted it to the person/client, what its intent is with the person, and what it gets from the relationship. At some point during the conversation, ask the name of the entity's mother (if she's not dead, it will know that fact), grandmother, or other deceased loved one. If the spirit entity cannot remember a name, which is rare, you may request the invisible world of Spirit: "I ask for the loved ancestor of [entity's name] to come to the portal of light to receive [entity's name.]"

7. Ask the spirit entity to look up toward the ceiling, "where there is a bright light opening up like a doorway, a portal to the Upper World, to Heaven." Ask it if it sees the light. When it answers affirmatively, ask it if it sees a hand reaching from the light. Ask it to identify whose hand it is (usually, it is the loved person they named earlier, but sometimes there are surprises, such as the presence of Jesus or Mary, etc.).

8. Ask the spirit entity, before it goes, if there are other, similar, entities around the client (by name). If so, which is usual, have the entity ask them if they will go with it, for the open window of opportunity will close shortly, and this is a chance for them to receive healing and be with their loved ones who have gone before them.

9. If the others agree, which occurs often but not always, ask the "spokesperson" spirit entity to take them all by the hand, then reach up and take its mother's hand. Then, in a command voice, say, "Go now to the light."

10. The healer can accompany them as psychopomp. Or, angelic beings that assist the archangel Gabriel, who manages the portals of light for incoming spirit entities, can be asked to escort the spirit entity or entities to the light. This provides some safety from interference by demons that may be loitering around the portal, attempting to seduce souls for the dark forces. Psychically, watch the spirit entities until they are in the light or journey with them to the portal.

11. Check (psychically or by pendulum) to verify that the client is cleared.

12. This sequence of dialogue with the attached spirit(s) can be used with any methods of depossession of spirit entities, particularly with the shamanic journey method, unless there is some purpose in the client's hearing information from the spirit entity.

Afterword

This book began with three examples of possible deep-level demonic possession: the terrorists of September 11, a mother who killed her children, and priests who sexually molest children. People consider these actions evil. To me, evil is a mark of control of the dark forces through the possessing demons. But the people in these examples and many others are unlikely to read this book or come to me for help. In fact, a characteristic common among people who are serial killers, rapists, and child molesters is their belief that they do not need help. These "darkworkers" have given themselves so completely to their dark side, have traded away so much of their upper soul, and have so disconnected from the higher power of God as to have forgotten that they have a light side. They believe their dark side is all they are. Until they remember that they have a light side, their possessing demons will drive them through this lifetime — and possibly the next, and the next.

The world, however, is changing. The Christ-consciousness power of the sixth chakra is growing in humans, helping people remember who they are. We are being aided in this by the "indigo children," those who know who they are and why they are here. Books such as this remind people that there is self-help for unfamiliar and bizarre situations and symptoms, such as having a demon or a number of souls of dead people attached to your energetic body. And more and more people are learning (remembering) that, through the inner journey, answers can be found for the supposedly unanswerable existential questions, "Who am I?" and "Why am I here?" and "Who are all these others?"

People can remember their life purpose, the reason their soul desired and volunteered to return again to Earth. This inner journey of discovery can be guided by those such as I who practice pre-life regression, or the shamanic journey, to the space-time before this life, when the life contract, including soul's life purpose, was being written. Finding that you are the author of the challenges in your lifetime of illness, demons, handicaps, crises, and catastrophes — that others are not to blame — can be a shocking expansion of consciousness. You may discover that those were essential catalysts to your growing into who you are. Without them, you would not have developed the insight, compassion, caring, and unconditional love for people in similar plights.

The light being spread by all those who are doing their best to walk the path of their life purpose, being who they came to be, their powers supplemented by their connection with the higher spiritual power of God, is making the contrast with the dark, the demons, the darkworkers, ever more distinct, so that the dark forces are becoming more clearly and openly known. As this light reaches those who have been hidden throughout the millennia, some are fighting even more determinedly to survive and to remain hidden. Some, however, are having awakenings of their light sides. During the past year, first the fallen angels, and more recently several giant demons, have admitted to me that they feel somewhat badly about pain they are causing the individual they are attached to; and feel a growing interest in working for the "light" (which is the reason for the "womb of transformation.") This indicates a basic weakening in the structure of the "hive" of the dark forces, the point being that because something has always been does not mean that it always will be. Even though your life may have always seemed one of depression or illness, each new moment offers you a way to create something different. Turn off your television (especially "news") for a week. Call on the angels for help. Find your life's purpose, and awaken to the possibility of feeling joy and passion about life.

Index

About the Author

John Livingston is a practitioner of depossession and exorcism of parasitic demons, spirit entities, and dark ET's; of shamanic healing; of pre- and past-life regression; and of energetic healing ("Reconnective").

Born in the Queen of the Angels Hospital in the City of Angels (Los Angeles, Calif.), he grew up in the Sierra Nevada foothills east of Sacramento. John has been a surveyor, equipment operator, draftsman, field and supervisory geologist, consulting geologist, water-well dowser, marriage and family therapist, and clinical hypnotherapist. He holds a bachelor's degrees in Geology from the University of Southern California, and a master's degree in Counseling from Chapman University.

In 1995, John closed his businesses of consulting geologist and part-time counseling to find some way of being more in service to people. Following a spiritual odyssey, he began the study and practice of shamanic healing using core and indigenous practices. Although his first depossession or exorcism of a demon occurred with a client in a therapy sesion in 1977, this did not become a major part of his practice until 1997.

At present, John's time is divided between a client-healing practice both face to face and by phone "at distance;" writing self-help books about healing, and teaching classes on the nature of parasitic spirit entities, demons, dark and reptilian ET's and angels. Email: JohnL@john-livingston.com.